Journey to a Better Land

Nancy Berthiaume LaPierre

TEACH Services, Inc.
P U B L I S H I N G
www.TEACHServices.com • (800) 367-1844

World rights reserved. This book or any portion thereof may not be copied or reproduced in any form or manner whatever, except as provided by law, without the written permission of the publisher, except by a reviewer who may quote brief passages in a review.

The author assumes full responsibility for the accuracy and interpretation of the Ellen White quotations cited in this book. Unless otherwise indicated, all scripture quotations are taken from the King James Version of the Bible.

Copyright © 2021 Nancy Berthiaume LaPierre
Copyright © 2021 TEACH Services, Inc.
ISBN-13: 978-1-4796-1184-3 (Paperback)
ISBN-13: 978-1-4796-1413-4 (ePub)
Library of Congress Control Number: 2021901601

Scripture texts labeled (NKJV) are taken from the New King James Version®. Copyright © 1982 by Thomas Nelson. Used by permission. All rights reserved.

Scripture texts labeled (KJV) are taken from the King James Version of the Bible. Public domain.

Original advising and editing done by Peggy Paine, friend of the author.

To Memere and Mom

Foreword

This book is not only a family heirloom. It is also a light that shall shine in the lives of all those who read it.

Susan Berthiaume

Preface

"Nancy, you need to put all this down in a book!" Over and over I kept hearing my friends say this to me as I shared my experiences with them. I always responded, "I would need a loud wake-up call from God, asking me to write a book. I could never do something like that!" The wake-up call came through my son, Tim, and I found myself sitting at the computer thinking, "Lord, help me!" As I began writing, the memories started to flow, and I knew He had heard my prayer.

I am hoping as my story unfolds, you will have a powerful sense of God's loving presence. He is there through all of our situations. There is nothing too hard for Him. No matter how dark and hopeless life may seem, and it feels like you are about to drown, just remember to reach out for His hand, and He will always be ready to catch you and raise you up! Just reach out your hand...

Acknowledgments

My husband, Mark, is a mentor of deep meaning to me. My three precious children taught me patience, understanding, kindness, and self-control. Dear friends, who are like family to me, provided much encouragement. Finally, Peggy, thank you for countless hours on the phone editing this manuscript. God chose you for this task, and I am grateful you responded to His call. God bless and keep you all.

Contents

Chapter One—The Music 13
Chapter Two—Memere (Grandma) and Pepere (Grandpa) 15
Chapter Three—A Mother's Heart 19
Chapter Four—Dad 21
Chapter Five—Jesus in my Heart 24
Chapter Six—Following Jesus 26
Chapter Seven—Mark's View 28
Chapter Eight—The Choice 29
Chapter Nine—Our Beginnings 31
Chapter Ten—Family 35
Chapter Eleven—Fixy and the Green Pepper 38
Chapter Twelve—Putting the Children First 40
Chapter Thirteen—The Bus 42
Chapter Fourteen—The New Baby 44
Chapter Fifteen—New Hampshire 47
Chapter Sixteen—Protection in the Midst of Calamity 49
Chapter Seventeen—Healing and Sam Spade 52
Chapter Eighteen—Learning to Count it all Joy 54
Chapter Nineteen—The Sign 56
Chapter Twenty—Maine 57
Chapter Twenty-One—Our New Home 59
Chapter Twenty-Two—Meeting God's Family 60
Chapter Twenty-Three—Aaron's Decision 63
Chapter Twenty-Four—Timothy and Andrew 64
Chapter Twenty-Five—School Daze 65

Chapter Twenty-Six—Watch Care for Timothy and Promises for Aaron 67
Chapter Twenty-Seven—The Better Way 69
Chapter Twenty-Eight—Growing Boys 71
Chapter Twenty-Nine—The Card 73
Chapter Thirty—College Days 74
Chapter Thirty-One—Tennessee 76
Chapter Thirty-Two—The Opening Door of Providence 78
Chapter Thirty-Three—Life Changes 81
Chapter Thirty-Four—Caring for Mom 82
Chapter Thirty-Five—The New Job 84
Chapter Thirty-Six—Leaving Maine 86
Chapter Thirty-Seven—Waiting on the Lord 88
Chapter Thirty-Eight—A Home at Last 90
Chapter Thirty-Nine—On the Move Again 92
Chapter Forty—The Home God Chose 94
Chapter Forty-One—Transformation Needed 96
Chapter Forty-Two—Mom 98
Chapter Forty-Three—Forgiveness 100
Epilogue 103
The Better Land 106
Scriptural Index 107
Bible Studies 110
Recommended Reading 111
About the Author 112
Other Books by the Author 113
Reviews 114

CHAPTER ONE

The Music

Why are you cast down, O my soul? And why are you disquieted in Me? Hope in God, for I shall yet praise Him for the help of His countenance. **Psalm 42:5**

I awoke to the melody of the music that was so familiar to my ears. Uncle Sandy was playing the violin, and then the accordion, other adults were playing the spoons. Mom, and whoever else wanted to join in with her, was singing. They were singing those beautiful, old hymns in our French-Canadian style. Our whole family was saturated with this music, and many nights were spent in this manner. I listened, hoping tonight would end with the same peacefulness I now felt. I knew Dad was not enjoying the evening with them. He would go into another room and drink and watch TV. Actually, they'd all be drinking, but in the early evening they were mellow and happy. As the night wore on, and the drinking in both rooms continued, that relaxing music transformed into loud, angry voices. My fingers tightened on the blankets as I heard my dad emerge from the other room hollering and yelling. Like all the other nights, what started out warm and inviting, would end in terror for me and my brothers and sisters.

My home was a pretty scary place in the daytime, too. Every day Dad would come home after working hard and begin drinking until he became drunk. When he did that, he was very mean. Sometimes he tried to hurt us, especially my younger brother, Dennis. I'd take him to my room and put the dresser in front of the door, preventing Dad from coming in.

Mom was too wrapped up in her own little world, a hurtful one, to respond to what was going on with us. She'd go off with my dad's brother whenever she found occasion to, which only contributed to my dad's anger.

My other brother and sisters each handled life in our home differently. Many times my older sister, Millie, had trouble sleeping due to her anxiety. She found herself living on aspirin to stop the uncontrollable shaking. Often she had to deal with our dad and his behavior. One Saturday night when she was twelve years old, the neighbors came over and knocked on our door. They told us Dad was at the bottom of the stairs drunk and asleep. Millie went down and literally dragged him up the three flights of stairs to our apartment. She was forced to take 'Mom's position, and I assisted her in the care-taking of our family and home. Mom was constantly calling for me to rescue her. It seemed like I was always sleeping with one foot out of the bed, ready to run to her aid. Life was difficult. My younger sister, being small and fragile, was protected by my parents no matter what condition they were in.

> *As you can see, my childhood was surrounded by much darkness and my mind was filled with fear and anger*

As you can see, my childhood was surrounded by much darkness and my mind was filled with fear and anger. I knew I did not want any children I might have to experience what was happening to us. I often asked God, "Why do we have to go through all of this?" Asking that question one evening I became aware that it didn't have to be this way. I was deeply convinced and determined to find a better way to live, but I was not sure how. I needed to keep that peaceful music in my heart, and never let it end in terror again.

CHAPTER TWO

Memere (Grandma) and Pepere (Grandpa)

If you love Me, keep my commandments. **John 14:15**

The lifestyle I just described did not begin in my generation. My dad had a similar childhood to ours. His mom, Regina, was raised in a strict, Roman Catholic home in Canada. Her two aunts were nuns. She always loved and respected them and wanted to follow in their footsteps. When she was ten, her aunts came for a visit. While they were there they discovered how much Regina wanted to become a nun and suggested she leave with them. You can imagine the excitement young Regina felt when her mom actually said she could go! Her dream was finally going to come true. Everyone was happy for her! They had no idea that it would be five long years before she could return home.

Life at the convent was not easy. She had a daily routine of cold baths at 5:00 A.M. to awaken the senses! Then she made beds, had breakfast, did a few chores and began school by 9:00 A.M. At the age of fifteen, she became a governess for two little girls. This just added to the already full schedule. She was never allowed to laugh or take a vacation and suffered from overwork. On top of all this, a priest tried to do inappropriate things to her. She was shocked and decided to go and tell her aunt, but as she approached her, her aunt told her some startling news. The priest, the very one she was terrified of, had asked if he could take her on a trip! Regina was stunned, and seeing her hesitancy, her aunt asked what the matter was. Regina called him a name, but her aunt did not believe her, and said she should not be talking that way about a man of God. She eventually blurted out the whole story and her aunt became furious with the priest. A short time after, the same priest came to pick Regina up to go with him. Her aunt eyed him in fury and said, "You will not touch any of my girls!" With that, she spun him around and sent him flying!

Things went from bad to worse. Her aunts started to criticize her, no matter how hard she tried to please them. It came to the point where she could hardly talk or even eat. One day her uncle and mother made a surprise visit to the convent, and when they saw the condition she was in they brought her back home with them. Little by little she started to return to her old, happy self again.

When the family moved from Canada to the United States, they found a nice place to live in Connecticut. Regina and her sister, Rose, started working in a silk mill. A day came when the boss announced they were all going to go to the beach. When they were there, Regina saw a nun who was smiling at her. After talking with her, she asked if she'd be able to live in her convent, still thinking God wanted her to become a nun. She stayed there for five years, only to become ill and return home again. A total of ten years had been spent, but to no avail. Now, at twenty years old, the dream of becoming a nun was quickly fading. Praying, she said, "Okay God, You don't want me as your nun? Then I'll get married and raise a lot of children for You!"

When the family moved to Rhode Island, she found a job in another silk factory. A friend who also worked there suggested she come over with her sister, Anna, and meet her husband's brother from Canada, for maybe he would be interested in one of them. Alcide was a handsome twenty-four-year-old, and she was instantly attracted to him. At the dinner table his eyes kept meeting hers. How surprised and happy she was when he chose her to escort home. They continued seeing each other and eventually married. Their marriage was solid as they shared the same faith. Six little ones were born, fulfilling Memere's promise to raise a lot of children for the Lord. Pepere supported them by doing carpentry, painting, and playing his violin.

When Regina became ill again, and thought she was dying, she asked her mother to read from the Bible. Her mother was the only one in the family who had one. The Roman Catholics believed if you read the Bible by yourself, without the priest's interpretation, you would turn against God. So her mother said, "No," for she was afraid. Regina said, "How can this be? Would the book of God lead us away from Him?" Shortly after this a Protestant man came by their home and began sharing religious tracts with Regina's children. They gave them to her and she read them. When her mother found out, she was very upset, and waited for the salesman to come back. She told him not to leave his papers with them anymore. The salesman was not intimidated and said, "You know, your Catholic Bible is the same as ours." All of a sudden her mother got the idea of converting this man into a Catholic. She got excited and let him go about convincing her. They decided to read different texts from his Bible and compare them with hers. She found out the texts were the same!

Regina was confined to her bed, very weak, but she was near enough to hear what was going on. She realized the salesman was telling the truth, thinking, "How can this be? We have been taught the two Bibles are different." She sprang out of bed, forgetting her weakness, eager to talk to this man! After all, hadn't she spent ten years in a convent? She'd show him a thing or two! As she stood there, her mother waited for her to say something for their defense, but nothing came out. They just could not find one difference between the Bibles. Questions instead of answers started whirling through their minds. All of a sudden her mother looked at her and said, "Regina, you are up!" She quickly said, "Yes Ma, I am up! It must be God wants us to know about these things." God healed her that day.

They started studying the Bible and learning what God wanted them to know. God revealed to her family that His Law was holy, just, and good, like He was. They determined to obey God's Law as He had asked them to do in John 14:15, and began to worship on God's Holy day according to the commandment.

Exodus 20:8–11 says, "Remember the Sabbath day, to keep it holy, six days you shall labor and do all your work, but the seventh day is the Sabbath of the Lord your God. In it you shall do no work: you, nor your son, nor your daughter, nor your manservant, nor your maidservant, nor your cattle, nor your stranger who is within your gates. For in six days the Lord made the heavens and the earth, the sea, and all that is in them, and rested the seventh day. Therefore the Lord blessed the Sabbath day and hallowed it." They were eventually baptized.

However, her husband Alcide took a little longer to accept the newfound faith. He studied right along with them and became convicted, but his loyalties to his devout Catholic family stopped him from following through with his convictions. He knew his family would disown him if he left the Catholic Church. It took a whole year after Regina's baptism for him to take his stand. After being baptized, he was faithful for five years. He always carried his Bible everywhere he went. Those were the best years.

Unfortunately, the fear of his family's disapproval and disappointment weighed heavily upon him, even to the point of denying to them his newfound faith. His parents did not believe he was still Catholic and they told him, "You are not a man because you have lied. You should have stood up for what you believed!" My Pepere was never the same after that. He gradually spent less and less time going to church. He started drinking heavily and things went downhill quickly. The confusion and pain Memere felt caused her to back away from God for a while, but that did not last long. Her love for Him was too deep. Several times she fell ill, to the point of death, and each time God healed her. She wrote all of her experiences on notepads and put pictures beside her writings to illustrate them. She became a strong, positive influence in our family.

Chapter Three

A Mother's Heart

Preserve me, O God, for in You I put my trust. **Psalm 16:1**

Memere strongly wanted her children to know personally the love she had with Jesus. Many times she prayed for them. Fernand, her first-born son, who was always kind, became a hard-working businessman and started a nursing home. When he was young, World War II began and he found himself stationed in Normandy, France. Sometimes he had to go to Saeintandre, to do some interpreting. While there he met a young French girl named Micheline, who had a little boy named Michael. He fell in love and married her. When he was discharged he came home to America alone, and waited five months until the government paid for all the GI brides to come and join their husbands.

At last they started their life together and had a lovely little girl named Miriel. Fernand did come to know and love Jesus in his older years and he became even kinder. This would have given such joy to his mother, except by the time he made his decision she was in a nursing home with Alzheimer's. The family went to see her after his baptism, hoping to share the happiness, but she did not seem to understand anything that was going on around her. Tragically, Fernand died in a car accident, but she will see him in heaven someday and it will be the best family reunion ever! All her pleading tears will then be transformed into rejoicing.

Raymond, or "Sandy," was her second child. He was called Sandy because of the color of his hair. He gave away whatever he had and was the life of any party, entertaining, and full of fun! He was one she prayed for intensely as he took after his father and his drinking ways. One night, he was coming home from playing his violin for money at a bar, when he decided to make a stop at his girlfriend's and convince her to go out with him and drink some more. He was already drunk, and it was well into the night. She didn't want to go, and while he was there, he died of a heart attack. This was long after Memere had died, sparing her the grief of his decisions and loss. God had tried to reach him. On Sunday mornings he would watch the preachers on TV and his eyes would fill with tears. He was survived by Raymond, his only child from a previous marriage.

Theresa (Terry) was her third child. She welcomed Jesus into her heart and life and her influence in the family was positive and sweet. She married a Christian man and they raised their children: Linda, Jimmy, and Joanne to know the Lord.

Next to be born was Roger, my dad, but I will share more about him later. The little baby girl who arrived after my dad also had a fun-loving disposition. Sadly, the addiction to alcohol was to be strong within Jeannette as well and being not healthy and often in pain, she also became addicted to her medications. She married a man who was not a Christian and they had two boys, Emile and David. After a tough life experience, she turned to Jesus and made her peace with Him, serving Him the best way she knew how. Her memory began to deteriorate and Emile cared for her in his home. When she got worse, he knew she needed a nursing home, and she seemed to be content there.

When Memere got pregnant with her sixth child, Pepere claimed the child was not his, which was not true at all. She was devastated that he would say such a thing and went to see a doctor to try to abort the baby. In those days abortion was different than it is now. The doctor gave her a bottle of medicine, which cost $10.00, and told her to go home and drink it. I don't remember what it was he gave her, but it was supposed to start the abortion process.

One day she held the bottle of medicine and fell to her knees, crying and praying to the Lord, asking Him for guidance to know what to do. A neighbor came over to the house to see her. She told her the whole horrible story. They got on their knees together and opened up God's Word, and God brought them to the text in Jeremiah 1:5. It said, "Before I formed you in the womb I knew you, before you were born I sanctified you, and I ordained you a prophet to the nations." The neighbor turned to her and said, "What are you going to do now?" They prayed again and she grabbed the bottle, went out on the porch, and threw it as far as she could. It landed on a rocky ledge, smashing into hundreds of pieces.

Her son, David, turned out to be the gentlest Christian man, and a minister for the Lord. He married a devoted, Christian woman named Cathy, and they were blessed with three children: Marina, David, and John. Thank You God, for bringing her neighbor just when she was needed most.

Chapter Four

Dad

Behold, I stand at the door and knock. If anyone hears My voice and opens the door I will come in to him and dine with him, and he with Me. **Revelation 3:20**

When Dad was young, he listened to Memere and always carried his Bible wherever he went. He met his bride-to-be for the first time when she was fifteen and he was nineteen. He joined the military for two years and was stationed in Germany. When he completed his duty, he was a totally different man. He had taken up drinking and smoking. He began dating Mom and they decided to get married despite their different religious backgrounds. Mom was Catholic and the ninth child born into a family of ten. She was not close to them and we never had much contact.

Nine years after their marriage, they realized their need of help beyond their own strength, as Memere was always sharing her faith and praying. Dad stopped drinking and smoking, and they made their commitment to Jesus, joining the church. They had a few years with God in the center of their relationship and home became more loving. We were happy going to church as a family. My older sister was six and I was four. However, as time passed, it was getting more difficult for Dad as two more babies had arrived, and we were never very quiet. Dad couldn't handle it.

When he found a job working at Fairmount Foundry, welding, he met people there who were not Christians, and he started to hang around with them. They asked him to go places and drink. If he said, "No," they'd say he was henpecked and did everything his wife told him to do! My dad didn't want to be known as that! He started to go with them, and we all stopped going to church as a family. Sometimes dad's brother, David, took us and we had fun-filled afternoons with Aunt Terry, Uncle Paul, and our cousins.

Drinking was such a curse in our family. One day my mom, twelve-year-old David, and Sandy's wife were going to a little variety store to pick up some items, and had decided to take a short-cut to get there. As they were walking, they heard some children talking about a man in the woods. They were all very upset, thinking the man might be dead! They told David to go and check what it was all about. He was hesitant, but not wanting to appear fearful, he ran into the small, wooded area across the street from where they lived. He found a man dressed in overalls like his father wore. Yes! It was his father, and there right beside him, was the hated bottle. He quickly ran to tell them. They were shocked, turned around, and ran as fast as they could to tell the family. It looked like he had become drunk again and probably had a heart attack while trying to make his way home.

> *As they were walking, they heard some children talking about a man in the woods. They were all very upset, thinking the man might be dead!*

A few days prior to this incident, Pepere had come to Memere before going to work, and had told her how sorry he was for what he had put her and the children through all these years. He acknowledged he was the one in the wrong. He told her he loved her, and went away that morning shaking his head and saying, "I am so sorry." He knew the truth, and how God wanted him to live, but the rejection of his family was too much for him. In the end he just could not get away from the bottle, no matter how sorry he was for everything. At fifty-eight, he ended his days alone, drowning his convictions with alcohol.

Several years after Pepere's death, Memere married a man who seemed to offer the hope of a better life than what she had before. He promised he would put her son David through college to prepare him to become a minister, but it didn't happen. George turned out to be not what he seemed. Bitterness grew into hate in the heart of my dad towards his new step-father and one day after work he decided he'd go and see them. Of course he paid a visit to the local bar first and was drunk when he arrived at their place. Thank God, no one was there at the time because my dad broke in through a window and went crazy! He threw all the furniture he could pick up over the porch railing of their third story apartment. Something evil had come over him and given him strength he never had before.

We did not live far from Memere's apartment, and when Dad did not come home that night, Mom sent my older sister and me to look for him. It was getting dark and my sister and I were laughing. We weren't feeling concerned as Dad not coming home was familiar to us. We arrived at Memere's apartment and knocked on the door, but no one answered. We went to the porch and found the window broken! Well, being young and not understanding the danger, we climbed in. We walked around the kitchen and seeing nothing unusual, we climbed back out and went home to tell Mom what we saw. The darkness kept us from seeing the furniture and stuff sprawled all over the lawn.

We later learned that my dad had been asleep in the living room and the police told my mom if we had found him and disturbed him, we might have been killed. They also told her my dad needed mental help, but she refused to believe what they said, and nothing was ever done.

Through all this, God was watching over us. My older sister summed up what we went through in a very accurate light. She said it was like living in two worlds: one foot in God's and one foot in Satan's. Thinking of it that way brings back to my mind a vivid picture. Memere had related to me a dream she had while she was staying with my parents. She saw my father sitting in his chair smoking, drinking, and watching TV. Jesus was standing outside the window, looking at my father with big tears running down His cheeks.

Chapter Five

Jesus in My Heart

Casting all your care upon Him, for He cares for you. Be sober; be vigilant, because your adversary the devil walks about like a roaring lion, seeking whom he may devour. Resist him, steadfast in the faith, knowing that the same sufferings are experienced by your brotherhood in the world. **1 Peter 5:7–9**

Memere always had many experiences to share with me, and I loved going to her home and listening. She made God real and personal. I relied on her in the midst of our chaos for all the guidance I could get! Whenever I had a problem, I would go and see her and she'd pray with me. She opened God's Word and He would answer her! I trusted her completely and always received such reliable counsel. I started to know for myself how much He cares for all of us. I began to see Him more and more in my life as I grew older.

I studied several Bible lessons through the mail and completed them all. I was eager for them to arrive, and enjoyed my time studying. As God showed me His truths, I was learning how to make my life different and was hungry for more!

One day a man came over to our house selling Christian books. I begged my mom to buy The Bible Story set of ten. It took a little persuasion, but she finally gave in and bought me the much-coveted books. I was so happy and thankful!

I read all of them to my brother, Dennis, explaining everything I could, telling him there was more to life than what we were seeing here at home. There was a loving God watching over us and He cared that we were hurting. My little brother always listened to the stories, and at last we had a place to go and get away from the hurtful surroundings of our lives. When we would sit together and read, we were brought into a quiet place. Thank you, God, for touching my mom's heart and influencing her to say, "Yes, we can buy those books." Now I had my Memere and those wonderful Christian books to go to, and find the peace I desperately needed.

I was baptized at the age of thirteen along with my two cousins, Jimmy and Linda, Aunt Terry's children. Millie had been going to church with me, but for some reason wasn't able to attend my baptism. I was extremely happy when I got home, but the rest of the family did not share in my joy. After I was baptized, I would sit at the old upright piano, teaching myself the hymn, "My Jesus, I Love Thee," which was my commitment to God to love Him forever. To my dismay, my parents sold the piano for money.

Review and Herald Publisher of the SDA Hymnal

Copyright1985

Chapter Six

Following Jesus

Show me Your ways, O Lord; teach me Your paths. Lead me in Your truths and teach me, for You are the God of my salvation; on You I wait all the day. **Psalm 25:4, 5**

At seventeen years old, I wanted to be re-baptized as my commitment to Jesus had deepened. When Millie told me she'd been studying the Bible and was going to be baptized, I thought it would be delightful to share that experience with her, and to have one sibling who wanted to follow in Jesus' footsteps! What a special day for both of us.

One particular memory stands out in my mind. My sister and I were deathly afraid of water. I had obviously forgotten about that part, when I was baptized at age thirteen, or I might have thought twice about doing it again. Our minister was doing the baptisms and he was unaware of what was in store for him. Millie was to be baptized first and did he have a hard time with her! Her feet were going everywhere as he was trying to put her under the water. Then after all that work with her, I came marching in. He had the same problem with me! He said he was exhausted when he got done baptizing us! Since then he always remembers to ask first if the one he is baptizing is afraid of water. Then he recounts the story to everyone with much laughter, saying how funny we looked with our feet in the air, thinking we were going to drown!

Shortly after our baptism I started seeing a young man who was attending college and planning to be a Baptist minister. We dated for four years and I loved him. Then for some reason, unknown to me, he broke it off. I was devastated. It was Christmas, the worst time ever for breaking hearts.

In February my brother invited me to some Bible studies he was attending. He figured I needed the change. I started to go and met some nice Christians my age. They did not believe as I did, but just being around young people who loved Jesus was enough for me. It helped me forget my troubles.

I went for a few weeks, but I was starting to feel the conviction I did not belong there. I had found the joy of keeping the seventh day holy, as God had asked me to do in the fourth commandment (Exodus 20: 8–11).[1] I tried to share this joy at the Bible study, but they did not want to hear it. I struggled with what to do. In the night I had a dream. I saw the finger of God pointing to a huge plaque with the Ten Commandments written on it. On one side I could see a dark figure, like a shadow looming over me. I remember looking at the evil figure and then at the finger pointing. When I woke up I knew what God wanted me to do. He wanted me to stand for His truth which was light and not choose the darkness (John 14:15, 21).[2]

I went back to the Bible study with a different perspective. This was going to be my last time. We were sitting around talking before we started, when there was a knock on the door. It was Rick with his friend, Mark. Mark said he wanted to learn more about Jesus. Everyone was delighted to have a new member with whom to share Him!

We began our Bible study and when it was over, Mark looked at me and said, "Do you want to get married?" He didn't even know my name! I said, "Sure," thinking he was just kidding. The Bible group then took a ring from a soda can and pretended to marry us. Mark and I talked a while and actually set an April date for the wedding! After all we were still just pretending!

I did not make that night my last for I wanted to see more of Mark. We were close in age, only four days apart and something about him drew me. I asked him, "Are you really searching for the truth?" He said, "Yes." I sent away for some Bible studies and started studying with him. He was digesting it all and believing everything God was showing him.

Chapter Seven

(Mark's View)

He who finds a wife finds a good thing, and obtains favor from the Lord. **Proverbs 18:22**

My grand parents on my father's side lived in Massachusetts. We would visit them often as I grew up. I met my grandmother on my mother's side, but my grandfather had died long before I was born. We'd visit with her occasionally. I had two brothers and one sister. My sister was the oldest of the children; I was the middle of the sons. My older brother and I did not get along well and my sister was too old to relate with me. I spent most of my time with my little brother, Peter.

My father brought us to the Catholic Church when we were growing up. I remember sitting in the church service and thinking, "That's the truth. That's not." My mom would stay home and make dinner for us. I thoroughly enjoyed those meals!

The summer after I graduated from high school I was involved in a car accident. I don't remember the accident or what led up to it. I was hospitalized with head and internal injuries. My younger brother, Peter, was killed.

Having a great interest in flying, I got into building model airplanes. I met a guy through the local hobby shop who was also a model airplane builder. Several of us would get together at my friend's house and work on our airplanes. That's where I met Rick. One day Rick's car was hit broadside by a driver who ran through an intersection. His car was wrecked, but he was not. Being now car-less, he asked if I could give him a ride to a local Bible study. I was glad to do so. He was surprised when I joined him in the study.

I met Nancy there. I said, "Hi! Want to get married?" She agreed to the proposition. Silly girl! She introduced me to Bible study guides and we would study together. I was baptized August 31st, 1974, and married on Sunday September 1st, 1974. There is a lot more to my story, but this is Nancy's book.

Chapter Eight

The Choice

A man shall leave his father and mother and be joined to his wife, and they shall become one flesh. **Genesis 2:24**

As **Mark and I continued** our Bible studies together we also started dating. I found out he had just broken up with his girlfriend, and we both made it clear, if either of our former loves came back, we would dump each other fast. So much for our wedding date in April!

Well, mine did come back around mid-March. He called and said he had to see me. He was delivering some furniture to my Aunt Terry, and wanted me to go along. I was torn because I was falling for Mark. My mom really loved Mark. While I was talking on the phone, sitting on the stairs, Mom was practically on top of me telling me, "No, don't go!"

In those days we listened to our parents, no matter how old we were and I told him, "No, I was busy." The relationship was over. I began to pray hard for myself due to the fact I was still in love with him. God answered my prayers in a big way.

Once again God gave me a dream. Mark, my old flame, and I were in a boat. Suddenly they both fell out and were frantically splashing in the water. During their attempt to save themselves they drifted away from each other. I realized I could only help one

> *When I woke up I knew without a shadow of a doubt who I was supposed to spend my life with*

back into the boat. I had to choose! My heart went out to my old love, but I automatically turned to Mark. When I woke up I knew without a shadow of a doubt who I was supposed to spend my life with. From then on I prayed the love I had felt for my other guy would be given to Mark. God granted my request.

He surely saved Mark for me. When he and his brother had the car accident, they were both pronounced dead on arrival, but the doctor gave Mark an IV. Peter died, but Mark regained consciousness. When he woke up he asked the doctor, "Do you usually pump blood into dead people?" The doctor answered, "No, but I was strongly impressed to do it to you!" He received 376 stitches in his head and his kidneys were not right, but today he is doing well. We are thankfully growing old together.

The night Mark decided I was the one for him, we were at a dinner-theater with fancy cloth napkins. An expensive night out, all dressed up with suits and gowns. It was a first for me. During the play when everyone was quiet, Mark realized he loved me, and he would never leave me no matter what. He tossed his fancy napkin in the air and started singing loudly the song, "Hooked on a Feeling," by BJ Thomas, which has been our song ever since. We made a real date to get married. What a happy day!

The night before our wedding Mark and I stayed up until the wee hours of the morning preparing for everything. Mark had training as a florist and made all the flower arrangements, doing a beautiful job. My parents were also up all night, only they were busy consuming their usual amount of alcohol.

Needless to say when it was time for the wedding we were all tired and some were still a little tipsy from the night before. My dad walked me down the aisle, and I must admit it was actually me walking him down the aisle instead of the other way around! I literally had to keep him from falling. It was not a big event. My immediate family was there and a few of my favorite aunts and uncles. Mark's family was attending and also a few church members.

It may not have been the best of weddings, but it was the best marriage, ordained by God. We have been married over thirty-five years and still counting. I cannot imagine life without Mark. He is definitely my better half. "Thank you, God, for Mark."

Chapter Nine

Our Beginnings

You who fear the Lord, trust in the Lord, He is their help and their shield. The Lord has been mindful of us; He will bless those who fear the Lord, both small and great. **Psalm 115:11, 12**

Mark and I started our adventurous life together. We never did have a real honeymoon. We just stayed at my Aunt Terry and Uncle Paul's place for a while. Mark was a hardworking man. He and I worked together at a manufacturing plant. Then he decided he wanted to go to Atlantic Union College. We moved to Clinton, Massachusetts, to be closer to the school. I found myself a job to help with the tuition, but it was not in God's plan for us. I was laid off about seven months later and couldn't find any work. Mark had to quit school, and with disappointment we moved back to Rhode Island.

We knew God was in control and we waited on Him to tell us what to do next. One year later I found myself pregnant. After three months I lost the baby. It was a very sad time for us.

We rented several places in Rhode Island. Then God opened the way for us to buy a home in Connecticut. We had to wait a while because it was being built when we bought it. When it was finished we painted it high gloss, fire engine red and high gloss, white trim. We wanted everyone we knew to be able to find us when they came to visit! They would find us for sure with the only bright red house on the block!

Mark had a job bringing home $90.00 a week. It was possible to pay the car payment, mortgage on the house, and buy groceries, but it was hard to keep up. There was no money for electricity, so we used kerosene lamps and a foam cooler became our refrigerator. When it was cold we just put everything on the porch outside. To tell you the truth, we loved the kerosene lamps. We didn't like living without the refrigerator though! We also could not afford the heat. Mark got himself an old 275-gallon oil drum and made a wood stove out of it. He is so resourceful! With four-foot logs in the stove, we were nice and toasty warm.

Several months later I became pregnant again. It had been two years since the loss of our first baby. We were excited and prayed every day for a safe delivery. I was nauseous for the whole nine months, and needing extra care I went to live with my parents. I would have to say I had the worst pregnancies ever. I had been sick the three months I was carrying my first child and now I was going through it again.

I stayed with my parents just a short time. The only way I was surviving the fighting and yelling was to take my Bible and whatever other encouraging books I had and go alone into a bedroom. Meanwhile, my sweet husband was still at our home in Connecticut working, only coming to see me on weekends due to the distance. Not good! I stayed for about four months.

(Mark's Letter)

My dearest sweetheart,

I love you my honey and I hope you are feeling better. My heart is heavy in loneliness for you. I look forward to the day when we will go home together in the clouds and never again be separated by time and space. I love you so, that I feel like crying because we are apart. It is no fun coming home to an empty house and sleeping in an empty bed. When I come home I want to hug you but you are not there. I will come to you my dear as soon as I can. I give you all my love, my lovely one, for it is you who gives me a reason to live each day. How is it one as comely as you could love me? I am thoughtless and inconsiderate, thinking only of myself. I am not worthy of so great a gift as your love. For this I love you even more. So much I would give up all that I would ever have for you.

**To my darling,
I send my love,
Mark**

Coping better with the nausea, I returned to Connecticut. Right before my due date, we asked my younger sister if she'd come and stay with me for I needed the help. However, my due date came and went and it didn't look like I was ever going to have this baby! I often experienced false labor just to be disappointed. Then, three weeks after my due date, November 1st, little Aaron was born.

Birthday Story of Aaron Roger LaPierre
Aaron-meaning Mountain of Strength!

We waited three years for you to be born, so when you finally came we were ready for you! The year was 1977 and it was Halloween night. The pains began and started coming fast. I still passed out candy to the kids despite not feeling well. I really did not want to have you Halloween night, but knew when I went to bed you would be arriving soon.

It was about 5:00 A.M. when I woke your dad up and said it was time to go, but I still hesitated because I was afraid and went to visit a neighbor instead. I stayed a bit with them and had hot chocolate. Then we headed to the hospital which was a good half-hour away. Visiting the neighbor was probably not a wise choice, but we made it without any mishaps.

When we arrived, the receptionist asked what our problem was because I did not look pregnant, even though I was more than three weeks overdue! You arrived a few hours later. This was Tuesday and you were born at 10:43 A.M. weighing seven pounds, eight ounces and twenty inches long. To your dad and me you were beautiful.

Your grandparents, uncles, and aunts loved you very much. It was a real job getting through your first year with my family. All they wanted to do was hold you and they would never let you sleep!

Much of our time was spent at Memere's and Pepere's. Being the long awaited first grandchild made you very special. My family always knew you were going to be a boy, and even bought a little blue pair of pajamas with a football on it before you were born! I still have them to this day. You are a treasure to your dad and me.

We love you forever,
my sweet Aaron

(Mark's View)

It's a boy! We waited quite a long time for this one. Money is tight, but we have a crib and a changing table. We can do this!

Chapter Ten

Family

Fear not, for I am with you. Be not dismayed, for I am your God. I will strengthen you. Yes, I will help you; I will uphold you with My righteous right hand. Isaiah 41:10

Life was quite interesting after Aaron was born. Caring for a new baby was both exciting and challenging. Aaron was inquisitive which caused him to get into everything. Then when he was eleven months old, I found myself pregnant again.

Aaron was just starting to walk, and I am sorry to say, I had the same sickness I had for the last two pregnancies. It was hard to take care of him and be so sick. This time I was determined to stay at home. I taught myself the guitar which took my mind off my nausea, and with God's help I made it through.

One day, when I was praying for help and guidance, I took the Bible, opened its pages and was led to Isaiah 41:10. It read, "Fear not, for I am with you. Be not dismayed, for I am your God. I will strengthen you. Yes, I will help you; I will uphold you with My righteous right hand." I thanked Him for His immediate answer, again realizing He was watching over us as a family. I don't know how many times I have claimed that promise through the years. Our Father is an awesome God.

Memere came to stay with us for a while, which was nice. Just having her around was wonderful! She spent lots of quality time with Aaron.

Mark was now bringing home around $100.00 a week and money was still tight, especially with Aaron and a new little one on the way. I figured I better do something to help. I got my daycare license, and our home was always full of children! Exhaustion from doing this left me with little to give when my own baby arrived. I carried guilt about this for a long time, but the day came when I let it go, and accepted God's forgiveness.

My brother, Dennis, also came to stay with us during my pregnancy. He was fourteen years old and needing a change from living with my parents. We always tried to be a witness to him, showing him how to live right with God. He had a sweet spirit, but was having bad breaks. As he grew into a man, he started to make better choices, marrying Susan and raising two children, Matthew and Amber.

The time was getting closer for me to have our baby. Mark and I knew we had to do something with Aaron. By then my brother had gone back home and Aaron was twenty months old. We called my parents and asked them to come and get him. We figured we wouldn't have to be away from him too long, but again my due date came and three weeks passed! That was the hardest time for me. However, my parents had become loving grandparents and enjoyed having Aaron. Little Timothy was born July 19th, another special miracle.

Birthday Story of Timothy James LaPierre
Timothy-meaning Honoring God!

We chose your name because we wanted you to have a Bible name. Your brother was Aaron and your dad was Mark, so we had to keep the Bible names going.

The year was 1979 in July, a hot July! Believe me; I was ready for you to come! Around the middle of the month I cleaned and scrubbed the house all day, so I knew something was going to happen soon. I always got that way just before I went into labor. I was already more than three weeks overdue!

We had packed Aaron off with your grandparents three weeks earlier. It sure was lonely without him. Your dad would go to work and I'd be alone. I would talk to you all the time.

The night of Monday, the 18th, I went to bed tired, but happy and ready for anything. I started to have some pain, but just ignored it until 3:00 A.M. I knew by then it was time to get ready for the hospital because it was thirty minutes away. I always had a bad habit of waiting until the last minute to go.

We finally left around 4:00 A.M. Your dad must have been speeding because a policeman was behind us. He didn't pull us over, but just followed us. I figured he must have known something might be wrong because we were heading in the direction of the hospital. He disappeared after a while.

Our labor lasted until 7:42 A.M. I was having you naturally with no medications just like I had Aaron. Your dad was there helping me to stay focused on breathing with every awful, painful contraction. Just when I thought I could not stand another pain, out you came!

You were twenty-one-and-a-half inches long, eight pounds, four-and-a-half ounces with black hair and not a blemish on you. Everyone said how beautiful you were and we agreed!

We loved you so much. Your dad was quick to get up in the middle of the night to feed and change you. You are very special to us.

We love you forever,
my sweet Tim

(Mark's View)

He's not happy. He sounds like he's insulted by being dumped out into this world. We will just take him home and love him.

Chapter Eleven

Fixy and the Green Pepper

And all your children shall be taught by the Lord, and great shall be the peace of your children. **Isaiah 54:13**

Now we had two lively children to share our lives with. Despite the fact they were always thinking of new mischief to get into and being difficult to manage at times, it was also loads of fun! We enjoyed reading stories, taking walks, going on picnics in the woods. We loved going to the zoo. We were determined to bring them up in the Lord and give them a Christian education.

We became vegetarians when Aaron was two years old and he let us know he was not going to be happy living without meat! When it came to eating, I had trouble with him all the time. On the other hand, Tim just loved to eat, especially the sweet stuff. Mark and I were not in agreement about this. I was health conscious. Mark, on the other hand, was not. He would buy a cake or pie and take a knife, slicing it into four exact pieces, expecting us to eat our entire share, never saving for another day. I definitely had to keep him under control.

We lived in our little, shiny red house appreciating God's blessings. We were a happy family, not having much, but having each other and trying to do what was right in the sight of God.

We'd attend campmeetings in the summer at South Lancaster, Massachusetts. The boys just loved it and always had fun staying in tents for ten days! It was a big spiritual retreat, like being in church all the time and learning about God. We never missed a camp meeting!

We also had a family cat God gave to us in such an unusual way. One hot, August day, Mark and I needed some things at the store and decided to walk there with the boys as our family car was not running. Aaron was five at the time and Tim was three. We did not even think how long it would be to walk to the store with two little ones in the heat. We just went.

On the way there, my boys started to complain they were thirsty. Mark and I had totally forgotten to bring water with us. It was taking an hour to get to the store, and they were in trouble, with nothing to quench their thirsts. I began praying, "Oh Lord, what are we going to do?" Then right there in the middle of our pathway was a big, juicy green pepper. Talk about an answer to my prayer! Where did this pepper come from? We were not near any homes. To me this was God's answer to my kids' thirst problem. I picked up the pepper and broke it into pieces and gave it to them, which quenched their thirst just fine. "Thank you, God, for meeting my children's needs."

We got to the store, purchased our items, and headed back toward home. On the way, we passed by some woods and a little yellow kitten came running toward us. He was adorable! We figured maybe the mama had her litter in the woods and this little one managed to escape. Well, we did not see any sign of a house nearby or the mama cat so we just kept walking. The kitten followed us and of course the boys were thrilled! Every time we went to pick him up, he'd begin to cry, and we'd put him down. He happily continued with us, his little tongue hanging out because of the heat.

That little kitten stayed behind us all the way home. When we arrived, Mark said he deserved to live with us since he had walked such a long way in the heat

That little kitten stayed behind us all the way home. When we arrived, Mark said he deserved to live with us since he had walked such a long way in the heat. We called him James Fix after the famous runner. From then on Jimmy Fix, commonly known as Fixy, was our treasured new addition to the family.

One sad day he was hit by a car, but thank God he was still alive! We brought him to the vet immediately. They had to do surgery on his jaw and wire it up. Then we had to nurse him back to health, which was very challenging. It was a happy day when he finally drank by himself. Thank God we had our little Fixy back.

Chapter Twelve

Putting the Children First

Train up a child in the way he should go, and when he is old he will not depart from it. **Proverbs 22:6**

Memere came to stay with us again when Tim was two. Sometimes the kids were very hard for me to handle alone while Mark was working, and it was nice to have her with me. She was always praying for us and I know her prayers are what got me through the days. It seemed I responded to the boys better whenever she prayed. Even after she left, things were easier. I know God sent her to us when we needed her most. I learned we have to pray unceasingly when we are raising God's children.

Mark and I regularly attended church and always got involved by being leaders in the children's meetings and helping out in the Vacation Bible School. Mark was a deacon and we would put on the vesper services once in a while. We loved working for God!

Then came the day we realized our little house was too much for us. We were having a tough time making the mortgage every month. Aaron was six, getting closer to school age. We attended some classes on Christian education and the man said we couldn't afford to not give our children this opportunity. We became convicted about what God wanted us to do. We also knew it wouldn't be possible for us to pay for Christian school and keep the house too.

Mark had the bright idea of buying a school bus and living in it to decrease our expenses and have enough for the school tuition. He made it sound like fun! We would take the seats out; build beds, a shower and closets. We would also put a refrigerator and stove in it. We had a heater for those cold days and nights. It would be just like a big motor home when we finished.

We sold our bright red house and bought a seventy-two-passenger bus and took all the seats out except two in the front. We turned them so they were facing each other, and placed a table in the middle. Mark built bunk beds and the lower bunk opened like a chest for the boys to store things in. He made a closet on each side for clothes. We installed a refrigerator, stove, and gas heater. He built a shower and put a portable toilet in. Our bed was in the back by the emergency door.

The boys did not care for this change at all, especially our oldest. He hated leaving our nice home for a school bus. Tim was younger and adapted better, but it was not the best of times. Mark, however, saw some humor in it, calling the children "our little bus boys." This experience taught us well how to adapt and live without material things. I looked at it as getting us ready for the time of trouble, (Daniel 12:1)[3], and I still thank God every day for the huge step He convinced us to take.

CHAPTER THIRTEEN

The Bus

Great peace have those who love Your law, and nothing causes them to stumble. **Psalm 119:165**

(Even living in a school bus!)

Oh my, life in the bus. Where do I begin! Aaron was six years old and Tim was four when we moved in, cat and all. We were still in Connecticut. It was around March.

We drove the bus to a nearby campground. The snow was gently falling and it was very cold. Our little gas heater did not have any gas in it. We had hoped to get a propane tank when we got to the campground, but unfortunately it was too late when we arrived, so we spent the night freezing! It wasn't fun.

Early the next morning Mark left for work. I felt it was unfair for him to spend all day in a warm place, and I had to struggle here in the freezing cold with two little boys! We just bundled ourselves up and stayed wrapped in blankets. It was especially tough when the kids had to go to the bathroom as we had to venture out into the snow and cold to the restrooms.

We muddled through the day, attempting to be warm, reading and trying to have a good time. I always endeavored to keep my courage up by smiling and singing and being cheerful. The boys and Fixy did not seem to mind it at all. They were happy enough.

Mark came home around 5:00 P.M. purchased the much-needed tank, and we were warm at last! We stayed at the campground for about three months, which was long enough for Aaron to find plenty of trouble to get into. One day he managed to shut off all the electricity in the camp! That did not go over well with the manager.

Then he had the bright idea of taking all the stone fireplaces apart. Mark had to buy some stone and set out to rebuild the fireplaces Aaron had torn down. You can be sure little Aaron had to accompany him all night, being eaten alive by black flies. I would like to think he learned a big lesson, but I am sorry to say Aaron was still enjoying whatever his little hands and feet could find to do.

Around the middle of May we decided to move to another campground which was more pleasant. It was on a lake. The air was starting to warm up. The flowers were blooming everywhere. This new campground was a sweet place for us to be in the summer. We went on picnics in the woods and loved swimming in the lake. The boys had fun with their bikes, riding all around. Aaron was still finding things to get into and Tim was always following him, copying whatever he would do. Mark was occupied fixing his old Mustang and we settled down to enjoy our summer, having many happy Sabbaths there.

Then I found myself pregnant again. Oh no! What would we do now? The bus was not fixed for a new baby. Not much space in a school bus for raising two kids. Now we would have to figure a way to squeeze in one more!

Chapter Fourteen

The New Baby

You shall teach My words diligently to your children, and shall talk of them when you sit in your house, when you walk by the way, when you lie down, and when you rise up. **Deuteronomy 6:7**

Immediately Mark started to work on adding a new sleeping space above our bed in the back of the bus. It had to have a door to prevent the baby from falling out. The door had bars like a crib and a slide latch on each side to keep it securely in place. It was about six feet long; making it possible for our baby to grow and still be comfortable. It was a very nice bed.

The bus was finally ready for our new addition. My boys were excited! August came and Aaron was to start first grade. We decided to move just for the winter to have the baby and began searching for a house closer to the Christian school in New London. We found a summer home in Niantic with a lovely window overlooking the ocean. It would be more comfortable to have the baby there instead of in the bus.

> *"The angels witnessed the way I was disciplining my children, and they were weeping."*

As usual, during my pregnancy, I was often in bed, nauseous, and throwing up. The boys would mimic me and had their own throw-up bowl. They saw my disciplining as a game. Coming to the end of my rope, I'd find myself screaming, yelling, and smacking them on their shoulders or whatever was within reach as they walked by my bed.

I decided we all needed to calm down. There was a special promise box the kids and I read out of every day. We sat down and each took a promise and read it to each other, as well as the explanation on the back of the card. I hoped that would get them to be quiet, at least for a little while. They each took one and read it out loud. Then I took mine. I can't remember what the text was, but when I turned it over to read the meaning, it said, "The angels witnessed the way I was disciplining my children, and they were weeping." It affected me to think the angels were watching my behavior toward my children. I became very aware I was not alone, and I tried to be more careful with everything I did. Thank you God, for correcting me when I am doing something not pleasing in Your sight. You do not holler and smack me when I am wrong. You speak with a still small voice and Your heart hurts, knowing I am only harming myself and those around me when I am outside of Your loving will.

November came. Our baby was due around the fifth. I was getting a little worried about what to do with Aaron and Tim while I was in the hospital. We asked Cathy, the woman who drove Aaron back and forth to school, if she would take care of them. Thankfully, she said, "Yes." Now all we had to do was to wait. The fifth came and went. I kept thinking this baby was going to be three weeks overdue like the other two!

Big surprise! Three days after my due date, November 8th, little Andrew was born. He was our last, special gift. God had given us three beautiful sons to bring up in His ways.

Birthday Story of Andrew Steven LaPierre
Andrew—meaning Strong, Manly

We chose your name because it had to be in the Bible. We chose Steven for your middle name because of our dear friend Steven from New Hampshire.

Andrew, your father and I love you very much. You were my last baby. You were born on a Thursday at 8:55 A.M. in the Westerly Hospital, the same hospital as your older brothers.

Our labor began around 4:00 A.M. We called Cathy and packed up Aaron and Tim. They didn't want to leave us, but they knew they had to.

As your dad and I drove, the police came up behind us again, just like they did for Tim, only this time they followed us all the way to the hospital! When I got out of the car and the policeman saw me, he knew what was happening and said, "Good luck!" and left.

You were a good-sized baby, weighing nine pounds, five oz. You were twenty-two inches long and beautiful, just like your older brothers. We were all excited. You are also very special to us.

**We love you forever,
my sweet Andrew**

(Mark's View)

This one has a quiet spirit.

Chapter Fifteen

New Hampshire

You shall not take vengeance, nor bear any grudge against the children of your people, but you shall love your neighbor as yourself. I am the Lord. **Leviticus 19:18**

We brought Andrew home to the house on the beach, and stayed there until Aaron was finished with first grade. We found ourselves many times packing our children up and going to visit my mom and dad. They loved their grandchildren very much and my children loved them. Thank God.

We moved back to the bus in May, when Andrew was seven months old. He had a hard time adjusting at first to his new surroundings. He did not like his little bed Mark had built for him. When we tried to put him there to sleep, he would cry. However, it did not take him long to get used to it. After a while, when 6:00 P.M. came around, Andrew would always point to his bed and want to go in it, for which I was grateful.

One day we heard from Steven and Mary-Sue, some dear friends in New Hampshire. They asked us to come and live with them for a while. We could hook up to their septic system and have running water during the warm months. It didn't take us long to start the bus and move! We were glad to have friends close by.

We still enjoyed campmeeting during the summer. When we were in Connecticut it was in South Lancaster, Massachusetts. Now, living in New Hampshire, we went to Freeport, Maine, still going the week before to help set up everything.

Andrew was nine months old when we moved to New Hampshire. Aaron was almost eight and just starting second grade. Tim was six, not quite ready for first grade. We put Aaron in the Colin Blakeney Christian School and life in New Hampshire, in the bus with three children and Jimmy Fix, began.

However, life for our kitty, did not last long. He was always getting into a neighbor's yard, and they would come to the bus and complain about him. They said if our cat continued to be in their yard they would poison him! We were horrified!

We never thought they actually meant it, but it wasn't long before we found Fixy under the bus deathly sick. We brought him to the vet to see what was wrong, and sure enough he had been poisoned. He died and we cried. God knew who was responsible for this action; I just prayed that He would take care of it all.

Chapter Sixteen

Protection in the Midst of Calamity

God is our refuge and strength, a very present help in trouble.
Therefore we will not fear. **Psalm 46:1, 2**

It was encouraging to be near our Christian friends, but our two oldest boys were always finding some mischief to get into on their land. It seemed they were no better than our cat was! We would always hear of something or other they did wrong. The only difference between the cat and the kids was no one was threatening to poison them! We were thankful for that. Sometimes I wished we lived alone, away from everyone, and the kids could play and not upset people all the time.

Tim turned seven and started first grade. Aaron was nine and starting third. Now I was alone with Andrew and my days were a little less busy. I did have a car and I spent time visiting my friends. One of them had three boys like me, but they were home-schooled.

When Aaron was ten years old and Tim eight, they joined the Pathfinders, which is like the Boy Scouts, only affiliated with the Seventh-day Adventist Church. They got to do many fun things which kept their little hands and feet busy. There was not as much mischief going on at the bus anymore.

One mid-January morning we woke up to a misting, cloudy day. I remember thinking, "I have such a full day with much to do!" Mark said I needed to go shopping for some heating tape for the outside pipes. They were always frozen in the winter, but we still had to wrap the tape around them to keep them from breaking.

I also had lots of laundry to do, and with the laundromat next to the boys' school, I decided I would venture out, drop off the boys, and continue on my errands. The night before had been very cold and when it began to mist it caused all the roads to freeze and turn to black ice.

Driving down the big hill toward town, the road looked clear to me. I had no way of knowing it was black ice. I was only going around thirty mph, but on black ice that was much too fast! We started going all over the road, totally out of control, hitting another car coming toward us and slamming right into the snowbank.

No one in the other car was hurt. However, we did not fare as well. The little Pinto I was driving was totaled. Tim was in the front with me, and Aaron and Andrew were in the back seat. Aaron never liked to buckle up his seat belt and I was always on him for that. Well, true to form, Aaron was not buckled, and he went flying; his two legs going in different directions! He broke his femur which is the top part of his leg.

Andrew was in a car seat, but he slammed his head against the door. When I looked back, he appeared to be knocked out. He was two and a half years old at the time of the accident. Tim seemed to be alright, and he and I managed to pry ourselves out of the car. I looked around and felt like I was in another world. All my laundry, the kids' toys, and everything we had in the car, including my glasses, was now thrown all over the street. It was still misting and the world looked gray and threatening. Here is the story as it appeared in the day's newspaper:

"Rochester—Slick roadways combined with light snow and hail in Northern Strafford County early this morning caught commuters off guard. From about 7:30 to 9, police in Rochester and the neighboring communities responded to more than 25 accidents. Steady light rain turned to hail and the wet roadway to treacherous black ice. Most of the accidents in the area were simple fender benders, but police at the scene of a Barrington accident reported that two children had been seriously injured, one suffering a broken leg and the other facial injuries.

It took almost a half an hour for ambulances to reach the scene on Route 202. Toys, books, and debris from the cars were strewn all over the snow as one young boy lay huddled in a policeman's blanket on the snow. According to police, the driver of a compact car carrying the two children lost control while rounding a corner, hitting a snowbank before sliding sideways down the road, smashing into an oncoming car and ending up on the other side of the road. Both cars were wrecked, but no one else was seriously hurt." (Reprinted courtesy of *Foster's Daily Democrat*, Dover, NH)

Even though it was a half hour before any help came, it seemed to me only a few minutes. When the ambulance arrived it also slid into the snowbank! I was still feeling out of it and not sure what was going on. My neck was in awful pain and I found out later I had whiplash. Tim had a little concussion. He was nauseated for a while. Andrew had a severe concussion, and he ended up with crossed eyes for a month. It was the worst day of our lives. I was extremely thankful I never got into the car with my children without asking God's protection first. This whole accident could have been much worse. Thank God, not one of us died!

Chapter Seventeen

Healing and Sam Spade

Praise the Lord!!!!! **Psalm 148:1**

Aaron and Andrew were in the hospital for ten days. My Aaron was all strung up with weights to help keep his broken leg straight. My Andrew was getting better, thank God. He had to wear a patch over one eye to make the crossed one stronger. My Tim was doing well. We had some friends from the church that took care of him while we were in the hospital. The staff set up a bed near Andrew, enabling me to go between rooms and stay with both of them.

Jared shared the hospital room with Aaron and was also ten years old. He had been suffering with a fatal disease since birth and it was so sad to see him. He was a happy child, even knowing he would never leave the hospital. He appreciated being read to and I enjoyed reading Bible stories to him. His dad was in the same hospital with cancer and ended up dying while we were there. Jared died a year later. I admired his mom for her courage.

After a while we all went to stay with our friends from the church. The mom was such a sweet lady. We stayed until the boys recovered a little. Aaron had to wear a broom stick between his legs to help them grow properly. He also wore a body cast. Even with all that he still managed to get around quite well, and we were able to move back to our bus to carry on with our lives the best we could.

After four months his body cast and broom stick were removed. It was just in time for Easter in April. He had healed quickly! I asked the doctor if he had ever heard of someone in the same condition healing as fast as Aaron had. The doctor said it was all a miracle to him. I gave all the glory to God and His counsel regarding a healthy diet. I had prayed he would be standing on his own two feet by Easter Sunday, and praise the Lord, he was!

The boys went back to school and everything was just fine. On returning home one day, we found a yellow kitty sleeping in one of the beds! We knew the bus had several holes in it, making it easy for the cat to come in. My boys were delighted! He loved sleeping with my oldest son every night. We didn't even have to feed him. He would leave every day to go to the neighbors for food, and come back every night for the boys' love and attention.

It was not long though, before we started to feed him, and he decided to always stay with us. We named him Sam Spade, after the detective, because he investigated his way into the bus, into our lives, and eventually into our hearts. Now we had a yellow kitty again!

Chapter Eighteen

Learning to Count it all Joy

My brethren, count it all joy when you fall into various trials, knowing that the testing of your faith produces patience. **James 1:2, 3**

Living in the school bus was just as much of a challenge as ever. I would find myself getting disheartened. One afternoon I had brought the boys home from school, and they had to get ready for a Pathfinder function. We did not have much time and my boys were not cooperating very well. Aaron lost his temper when I told him he couldn't do something he wanted to do. I have always believed when we lose our tempers and get mad, we are inviting Satan into our hearts and homes. I tried to calm him down, but there was no calming him. Then I thought of what God said to do whenever we wanted Satan to be gone. I quickly said, "In the name of Jesus, get away from us!" My oldest looked straight at me, and all I could see was the whites of his eyes. He was pointing upward and screaming, "It is Jesus who is keeping us in this bus! He is the one that is discouraging you!"

> *I have always believed when we lose our tempers and get mad, we are inviting Satan into our hearts and homes*

Right then I took Tim and walked to my bed in the back of the bus, and knelt down and prayed for us. I felt like this was not my son talking to me, but Satan tempting me to be more discouraged. I told God I would not be discouraged anymore, and I would live in the bus for as long as it took and try to be happy about it. I did not want to give Satan his way. I would love God no matter where I was! My home was not here on earth, but in heaven. We have to make-do wherever God sends us, and try to be a witness always.

I got up off my knees, Tim still hanging on me with fear as a result of what he had just witnessed. We went to the front of the bus, passing by Aaron, who by now had retreated to his bed and was just lying there sobbing softly. We sat at the table, opened God's Word and while we were praying, Aaron crept quietly behind me and tapped me on the shoulder. "What is the matter, Mommy?" he asked. He did not remember anything of the incident. I then got up, and took them both to the back of the bus, knelt by my bed with them and prayed for our tempers. I asked God to take our anger away. Every time I was tempted to be downhearted, I remembered that night and things always looked better.

Chapter Nineteen

The Sign

Trust in the Lord with all your heart, and lean not on your own understanding; in all your ways acknowledge Him, and He shall direct your paths. **Proverbs 3:5**

I felt like the Israelites in the Bible. No matter how hard we tried to get somewhere, we just kept moving around in circles, never reaching the Promised Land. We had seen some acreage in Milton, New Hampshire, not far from where we were, and purchased about eight-and-a-half acres, thinking it would be nice to build a home there. We would pack picnic lunches, and go and stay there all day while Mark was digging a well. Those were fun days at the land. Then one day the neighbors told us we couldn't build on top of an Indian burial ground!! We hadn't known that and ended up selling it. Now we were back in the same situation, feeling no hope of ever getting out of the bus, until one night.

It was New Year's Eve. The cold of winter had settled in, and once more we were enduring frozen pipes; still using our friend's bathroom. Four-year-old Andrew had a real bad fever and was sleeping up in his little bed. Mark, the boys, and I were sitting around our small table talking and praying. We asked God for a sign indicating that things would get better for us. We were tired of living in the bus, and the boys were growing older. They definitely needed a change.

All of a sudden, the water started to come in spitting and crackling in the sink, like it does when spring comes and thaws all the ice away! We couldn't believe our eyes! We were seeing a miracle! The water was running, and we could stay in the bus instead of going down to our friends for our usual evening baths. We took it as our sign from God. The water froze again, after all it was January, but we had hope now!

Chapter Twenty

Maine

The Lord is good to those who wait for Him, to the soul who seeks Him. It is good that one should hope and wait quietly for the salvation of the Lord. **Lamentations 3:25, 26**

Someone told us about a Christian school in Norridgewock, Maine. It was called Riverview Memorial and it had ten grades instead of eight, like all the other ones we knew about. This meant our children would be home with us until seventeen years old instead of fourteen.

Norridgewock was a long way from where Mark was working in Kittery, Maine, but we went there anyway to check it out. We didn't know anyone, but I did have a church directory of all the churches, including Maine and their members. After praying, I looked up the church members in Norridgewock and chose one couple whose last name seemed easy to pronounce, as I was nervous making the call to people I didn't know! When I called Randy and Carolyn they were excited at the thought of having our two sons in the school. We were given a tour and introduced to some of the teachers. Everyone was pleasant. It seemed very clear this was the place the Lord had chosen.

We needed a place to stay in Maine until we could find a permanent residence to call home. Before we moved, we bought a nice little camper. Some friends of ours from the Rochester Church had sold it to us. Graciously, Randy and Carolyn told us we could park in their yard. We left the bus on our friend's land. Needless to say, it was easy to leave.

By this time Aaron was twelve, Tim was ten, and Andrew was five. We were all excited to be going to Maine! It seemed like we had learned all the lessons God had wanted us to learn while living in the bus. When we lived in Connecticut, my new home had caused some pride to take root in my heart. Living in the bus taught me that material possessions are not the most important things in this life. The day-to-day challenge of being there for six years gave us an experience of real value. We learned the true meaning of family and how to lean on God.

We arrived at Randy and Carolyn's in the early summer. School was not going to start until late August, giving us time to search for a place to live. We stayed with them for a little while, finding a campground not far from the school. How exciting for the kids! They loved campgrounds, but amazingly enough we had to live in a space even more crowded than the bus had been! Things tend to narrow and get more difficult just before deliverance.

CHAPTER TWENTY-ONE

Our New Home

And my God shall supply all your need according to His riches in glory by Christ Jesus. **Philippians 4:19**

We started to attend the Norridgewock Church and loved it! Word went out that we were looking for a house or someplace more suitable to live in before the cold winter of Maine was upon us. We met a couple from church who owned a mobile home park. They said we could choose a new mobile home from Indiana, and have it shipped. A spot had opened up, just perfect for us. We'd be buying the home and renting the land from them.

First, we would have to pick out the mobile home, and we had the fun of choosing everything in it, right down to the floors and walls! The shipment of the home proved to be a hard, long wait. We had chosen it in the summer and now it was already fall. The kids had started school and it was getting harder to heat the camper. The only thing we could do was pray. Maine is not a place to be in the winter months living in a camper!

Mark had stayed at the bus in New Hampshire to continue working, which meant we only saw him on weekends. Meanwhile, he was still looking for a job closer to us. Our home finally arrived in November, just before the holidays. They put it on a slab in the back of the mobile home park, near the woods. I thought it was just perfect. We had about three quarters of an acre and it was far enough away from all the neighbors. Now my boys and Sam Spade would have plenty of space to play!

The new home was spectacular! It had a fireplace, two baths and three bedrooms! We thought we were in heaven! It had come just in time before the real cold and snow hit. God is true to His promises.

Chapter Twenty-Two

Meeting God's Family

A man who has friends must show himself friendly, but there is a friend that sticks closer than a brother. **Proverbs 18:24**

We were overjoyed to be in a real house instead of a bus or a camper and then God opened the way for a new job for Mark at Bath Iron Works in Bath, Maine! It was about an hour and a half away. This meant we could be together again! Our church was only seven minutes from our home, and the boys' school was just a few miles. We couldn't have asked for better than this.

Mark and I started to get involved in our new church. We taught the Sabbath school divisions. When they asked me to be leader of Vacation Bible School, I agreed to do it and ended up being leader for quite a few years. It was easy to make friends from the church and school. One of them was Evelyn, the mother of Robert and Kristina. We always called Kristina our adopted daughter. The first time we met her, she was a cute eight-year-old who loved to eat apples.

I had been at home unpacking all the boxes from the move when Evelyn and her daughter came to visit. Kristina was eating an apple, and looking around, when suddenly something caught her eye. Inside a box were the curtains I had made for the bus. She loved them, and asked if she could have them. I gladly said, "Yes." Such a fond memory for me, the day Evelyn and Kristina cared enough to come and visit. Even after twenty years, we still call Kristina our daughter. She is a lawyer now and doing quite well. Robert, her brother, is an engineer. They were one of the families who have remained friends with us. Another was Lynda and her son, Bryan. They spent many potluck Sabbaths at our home. She has been like a sister to me.

Our first Thanksgiving in our new home was memorable. Renee and Henry and their three children, whom we had met from church, came to celebrate the holiday. It was snowing all day, but that did not bother us at all. We shared, laughed, and got to know each other. There was many a Christmas when Renee and one of her sons would dress up as elves and come knocking at our door, their hands filled with presents for our children. These are memories we will cherish forever.

Carolyn's sister, Barbara, and her daughter, Brenda, were a caring family. They were always there ready to lend a helping hand whenever needed. There were many loving people! They helped us get through the tough times of bringing up our children. Our families were too far away and the church and school became our family.

(Editor's View)

Nancy and Mark have been part of our lives since 1997. We met them when we began attending church in Norridgewock. Living an hour and twenty minutes from the church, we always wondered, "What would we do for dinner? Would anyone ask us over?" Going home meant nine hours between meals which wasn't going to work for us! I always brought food for dinner or a picnic in the car.

We soon discovered Mark and Nancy offered a big "Welcome" to their home every Sabbath and they meant it! Nancy was always bright and cheery and full of energy and fun. Mark was steady with both feet on the ground and smart. The door was always open wide and over the years, tummies were filled and many hearts warmed.

I watched them and what was going on in their home and often tears formed in my eyes because I knew I was seeing Jesus laughing and loving through Mark and Nancy. There was this deep, genuine, unbiased acceptance and energetic appreciation for every single person who walked through their door. There was healing and encouragement as a result. It truly was a place of refuge from the complexities and stresses of the world.

Chapter Twenty-Three

Aaron's Decision

Hear, my son, and receive my sayings, and the years of your life will be many, I have taught you in the way of wisdom; I have led you in the right paths. When you walk, your steps will not be hindered, and when you run, you will not stumble. Take firm hold of instruction, do not let go; keep her, for she is your life. **Proverbs 4:10–13**

We kept ourselves busy every day. I brought the kids to school and back, and did some house-cleaning to help pay the tuition. Aaron and Tim were making new friends and fitting in nicely. Five-year-old Andrew also made a friend. Phil was the same age and lived at the front of the mobile home park. He was such a cute kid and they both loved nature and all of God's creatures big and small, especially snakes and bugs. They had many happy years together, enjoying each other's' company. I was thankful he found a friend when we first arrived in Maine. Aaron and Tim were much older, and he needed to find someone his own age to hang out with. Andrew still keeps in touch with Phil, who married Kristen, a quiet, sensitive girl from Maine whom we have known since she was little.

> *"When a child wants to be baptized as badly as Aaron wants to, you better listen to him."*

Everything was going well for our family. When Aaron was twelve, the pastor came up to me and said he had requested baptism. I didn't think he was ready, but the pastor told me Aaron had been attending his Bible classes at school. He said, "When a child wants to be baptized as badly as Aaron wants to, you better listen to him." We then gave our permission, and our blessing. His friends were there and what a joyful day for all of us! Aaron was the happiest he'd ever been. Mark and I were thanking God.

Chapter Twenty-Four

Timothy and Andrew

Oh God, You have taught me from my youth; and to this day I declare Your wondrous works. **Psalm 71:17**

Several years later, Tim began taking Bible studies with Martha. She was a strong woman of prayer. She would come to the school and teach the kids Bible and religion. Tim made his stand to be baptized like Aaron, only he wanted it to be at the Sandy River. He was fourteen. Sabbath was a beautiful day. A few other kids decided to be baptized with him and a dear woman, named Phyllis, who wanted to recommit herself to God. Tim was smiling from ear to ear and we were praising God for another one of our children accepting Jesus as their Savior and Lord!

By this time Andrew was seven and had started first grade. His teacher was excellent and all the little ones just loved her! At the school, he met Bryan, who was four years older. They got along just like brothers, being interested in the same things, and it was a fantastic relationship for both of them.

I had been teaching Andrew at home since he was five years old. His teacher told us one day that he was bored, and she would have to put him in second grade by January. This meant Andrew would complete his first two years of school in one year.

During his first year, Andrew expressed an interest in playing the piano. There were two piano teachers at the school, Renee and Brenda. They both were inspiring teachers and he learned much from them. He always gave a terrific performance at the recitals, and we were bursting with pride! My other boys joined a choir called "The Witnessing Team," where the students would go to different churches and sing for God. They had such fun! All three boys were doing super, staying active at school for which we were deeply thankful.

Chapter Twenty-Five

School Daze

The end of a thing is better than it's beginning, and the patient in spirit is better than the proud in spirit. **Ecclesiastes 7:8**

Now my last baby was in school, and I thought it was time for me to finish my own education. I had stopped when I was sixteen years old to help my parents financially. I always said I would go back someday, and this was the perfect opportunity. It was only a few nights a week. It would take me four years to receive my diploma.

However, thinking about returning to school terrified me. I didn't see myself as smart enough, and the idea of sitting in a classroom with other adults was intimidating. Mark agreed I should go and promised to stay right by my side every step of the way. So encouraging to me!

After I enrolled, I said, "Wow! This is not going to be easy." I had three boys to take care of, a household to keep, and friends to help. I was also cleaning houses and the church to pay for the boys' tuition. Now I would have to add all the studying to my full schedule. Many times I questioned how I'd manage this overload.

When the first night of class arrived, I slipped into the back row as near the door as I could get, making it possible to run away if I had to without interrupting anyone. True to his promise, Mark sat right beside me. I was strengthened by his being there, but I still felt inadequate. Thankfully, the teacher didn't seem to have a problem with him accompanying me. The title of the course was "Self Confidence." What I learned kept me in my chair. It was what I needed to know before I could go on. Soon I was sitting up front, participating with the others and actually enjoying myself, but it was never easy with all the duties I had to perform day by day. I was going through life in a daze, inching my way to the finish line. Mark faithfully sat by my side for all four years, giving me his quiet strength and even teaching the math class on occasion!

Then came graduation night! My family and a good number of friends from church attended. As I walked down the aisle, and heard the shouts of approval and joy and pride in what I'd accomplished, I lifted up praise to God for His genuine love toward me and for the gift of Mark. They taught me how to take the first step, despite my fears, to value patience and the effort it takes to gain knowledge.

I love

Going out together

Going to classes together

Your strong moral support

Your smart mind

Your warm heart

Your gentle touch

Your loving nature

Your understanding

The pride you have in me

But most of all

I love you because

You are who you are

Kind

Considerate

Nice

Comforting

Faithful

Respectful

Loving

I find I can see God through you. I love you, my sweet husband. Thank you so much for being there with me through all situations and never putting me down for anything I try to do.

Chapter Twenty-Six
Watch Care for Timothy and Promises for Aaron

Rejoice always, pray without ceasing, in everything give thanks; for this is the will of God in Christ Jesus for you.
I Thessalonians 5:16–18

Tim finished his eighth grade and graduated at Riverview. He chose to attend Pine Tree Academy in Freeport for his last four years. We felt it was the best choice for him. Pine Tree was about an hour and a half away from us and he could live in the boys' dorm. He did well there, being very active playing his trumpet. By the time he was fifteen, he left the dorm and moved in with his friend, Jeff, and his family. They were faithful, Christian people and loved Tim as their own. Again, I was thanking God for His watch care over my children.

Aaron and Andrew remained at home. Aaron was sixteen, and he had a girlfriend from the school. She was Martha's daughter. I am sorry to say it was not a positive relationship for them. He dated her for about three years—three of the longest years we ever had to go through. Those two kids were struggling to find their way. I prayed diligently about the direction they were heading, and I thank God He heard a mother's prayer, and was watching over them. They ended the relationship and she eventually married someone else.

During that tough time with Aaron, I learned what praying unceasingly for our children meant. One time we were at campmeeting helping to set up camp. Aaron was looking forward to his girlfriend coming, but when she showed up, she was with someone else! He couldn't handle seeing them and caught a ride home from one of his friends. Mark went to find him and bring him back if possible.

I was upset, and retreated back to our camper to pray, and ask God for His guidance. I was crying to the Lord and praying for Aaron. I opened up the Bible, and asked God for some answers and encouragements. I was amazed when He brought me to Jeremiah 31:16, 17. It said, "Refrain your voice from weeping, and your eyes from tears; for your work shall be rewarded, says the Lord, and they shall come back from the land of the enemy. There is hope in your future, says the Lord that your children shall come back to their own border." What hope that was for me! God saw what I was trying to accomplish with my kids, and He was approving! I was encouraged and just had to share it with Terrie, a friend in the next camper. She prayed with me, and it did not seem long before Mark and Aaron came back. We prayed with him, and he seemed to be all right for the rest of our stay at campmeeting. Thank you, Lord!

Another incident we had with Aaron was when he decided to move out of our home and share a place with a few friends. Again, I was very upset over this because I thought his friends were not the best to be living with.

The day he left us, I went out on the back deck, and took my Bible and cried to the Lord and reminded Him of the scriptures He had taken me to before, how He was going to bring Aaron back to His borders. I told God this was my son, and I know He had told me to stop my crying, but how could I, when all this was happening? God again brought me to the scriptures, to Jeremiah 31:20, "Is this not My dear son? Is he a pleasant child? For though I spoke against him, I earnestly remember him still. Therefore My heart yearns for him, I will surely have mercy on him, says the Lord." What an answer! God promised this mother He would take care of Aaron. I was just to let go and let God. I did my best to do that, and Aaron was only gone for four days, and then he returned. Thank you, Lord! I know You will always be there for him.

Chapter Twenty-Seven

The Better Way

He has shown you, O man, what is good; and what does the Lord require of you, but to do justly, to love mercy, and to walk humbly with your God? **Micah 6:8**

My Andrew was doing great in school. One little girl in his class had been with him since first grade! Sandy was always sitting near Andrew, and always saying how much she liked him. By the time he was twelve, they were the best of friends. Andrew was such a happy guy. I guess you would have called him the class clown! Everyone enjoyed being around Andrew, including his teachers. They just loved him.

Tim told us about a job opening as dorm parents for the boys at the academy. Mark and I applied for the position and got the job! We packed our things and moved into the dorm. It was not an easy task to take care of seven boys, but with God's help we managed to do it! The bright spot was being able to have all three of our children with us for the year!

That May my dad died from lung disease as a result of all the years of smoking and the foundry work. Sorrow and relief filled my heart. Dad had been sick for a long time and I was thankful he was not suffering anymore. During my last visits with him, I noticed a real change of heart. He was sad for how he had lived his life and treated my mom and us. He became caring and soft, something he had not been for a long time.

> *How different was the home life my children had in contrast with my own childhood. The Lord had heard the prayer of my young heart and had shown me how to find that "better way to live."*

About four weeks later we learned the school was down-sizing, and our position was no longer needed. We headed back to Norridgewock, which made Andrew quite happy. Upon returning home, Andrew began taking Bible studies with Martha, who was also Sandy's grandmother. He wanted to be baptized in the river like Tim. He was twelve years old and we knew he was ready.

Andrew's friend, Knowell, requested baptism at the same time. It was another marvelous Sabbath day when we all went to the river to witness Andrew taking his stand for our Lord. After the baptism, we gathered at Knowell's home for a Sabbath potluck. The church members were there and it was such a blessed day! Again we were praising God for His faithful watch care and Andrew's joy.

How different was the home life my children had in contrast with my own childhood. The Lord had heard the prayer of my young heart and had shown me how to find that "better way to live." I could see the fruit of following His instruction all around me, a living miracle.

Chapter Twenty-Eight

Growing Boys

For You are my hope, O Lord God; You are my trust from my youth.
Psalm 71:5

Aaron always had a tough time with school, and finally stopped going and found himself a job. He quickly realized in order to do something with his life he would need to get his GED and proceeded to study for it.

Tim completed three years at Pine Tree and then transferred to Shenandoah Valley Academy in Virginia for his last year of high school as Jeff and his family were going to be moving there. They loved it and both of them successfully graduated.

Andrew was still at Riverview Memorial School with Sandy. As they grew into their teenage years, they became more serious about each other. They graduated from eighth grade together, and continued to do well for the next two years. When they finished their tenth year, they spent the summer in upstate New York selling health and religious literature which proved to be a meaningful learning experience for both of them. This reminded me of those two people who God sent to my family, selling literature which brought us out of the chaos and darkness we were in.

In the fall, the school board began a program called AE21 which means Adventist Education in the 21st century. Andrew and Sandy would be finishing their last two years of high school on the computer. Emily, who was Sandy's mom, was hired to be the teacher. The program proved to be of excellent quality.

When the kids were in their final year of high school, we had a tragedy happen. Our cat, Sam, died of Leukemia. He had been part of our family for fourteen years. Andrew and Sandy were on a mission trip when it happened. I felt terrible! Sammy had been Andrew's cat since he was little and living in the school bus. Actually, he started out as Aaron's cat, and then he was Andrew's. Andrew never got to say "goodbye." We all loved our little Sammy. God was merciful to him in his last days. He did not suffer at all. We brought him to the vet to see if anything could be done. The doctor said the cysts were too far gone. They just put him to sleep forever while he was under the anesthesia. It was such a nice, peaceful way. I was thankful. I had been claiming the Bible passage, Psalm 36:5, 6,[4] which tells us God loves the animals just as much as He loves us.

The kids completed their high school years and we put on a nice graduation for them. God saw our children through all their tough times of growing up and now they were ready to face the next step in their lives.

Chapter Twenty-Nine

The Card

Love never fails. 1 Corinthians 13:8

I was really feeling the emptying nest. After Aaron's graduation, he began to do some traveling. He lived in Texas, Missouri, and California. There were many concerns and prayers for him during this time. Europe finally became his home. While there he met his future bride, Sara, and they now have a sweet little boy, Jason. Mark and I have been to see them in Germany on several occasions and have discovered a whole new world. Our children often broaden our horizons.

Aaron has turned out to be such a caring, responsible family man. He has also expressed his love for us as he reflected on his growing years. There is one fond memory that stays in my mind. It was Valentine's Day and I received a beautiful card in the mail. I couldn't believe my eyes, for it was from my Aaron, who had never done anything like this before. He shared with us how he always remembered and missed the special times we had together, and all the long talks we used to have. He apologized for making me cry and told me how happy it made him that we never stopped loving him. He recalled one of the incidents when he ran away from home and Mark found him with his friends. Mark simply took them all out to eat and Aaron thought what a cool dad he had and came home. He thanked me for spending time with him when he had hurtful moments. He thanked us for taking such good care of him and for always making our lives fun, even when things were tough. Then tears welled up in my eyes as he repeated more than once how much he loved us and that we were the best mom and dad.

Chapter Thirty

College Days

Happy is the man that finds wisdom, and the man who gains understanding; for her proceeds are better than the profits of silver, and her gain than fine gold. **Proverbs 3:13, 14**

Tim graduated from the academy, and then went off for his first year at Pacific Union College in California with a full scholarship. At this time Aaron was living nearby and it was nice for the brothers to be together. That summer Tim worked at a camp in California, and met a girl he knew from his academy days in Virginia. Her name was Cali. They started dating, but then they stopped, realizing distance was going to be a problem as he was heading back to Maine. He was planning to be a French teacher and went to France for his second year of college. He had an excellent year there, and speaking the French language came easy for him. When the year ended, he went back to California to work at the same camp he had worked at the summer before.

For his third year of college, he received a scholarship for running and playing soccer at Columbia Union College in Maryland. He was excited, and off he went making many new friends. Then for the summer he came home, and worked at a camp near us. He was not sure what to do for his fourth year, but it did not take him long to decide to go off to France again! The following summer he came home to work at the same camp. Then finding out he needed one more year of college to become a teacher, he went to Southern Adventist University. He reconnected with Cali and they fell in love. Tim graduated with a BA in French and a minor in physical education and Cali was in the audience. He had worked long and hard for this and we were quite proud of him.

While they had been dating, Tim had made a scrapbook of all the special things he and Cali had done together. Sometimes they would trade off, and she'd put memorable things in it. It went on like this a few times, until Tim ended up with it. Well, during summer vacation in Florida, while staying with Cali's family, they went to Epcot Center for a late evening dinner. Tim chose a romantic spot near the water. While they were eating, Tim took the scrapbook out to show her how he had finished it. While they were both looking at it, Tim asked her to be his bride. Just as he was asking her, the fireworks began! She said, "Yes," and Tim was ecstatic! Now they could continue putting more things in their book, only this time they would be doing it together.

In the fall Tim was offered a teaching job at Shenandoah Valley Academy. What a time Tim had! He had wonderful college years, and now he was about to get married to the girl of his dreams. Their wedding was July 11th, 2004. What a day for all of us. Now I have two daughters to love. Tim and Cali have had two beautiful little girls, Madeline and Mollie. Mark and I are happy grandparents! We just love it!

(Tim's letter)

Mom,

Just wanted to send you a little note to say I love you very much and I would also like to say thank you for giving to the Lord. For giving Him all of your wonderful prayers for each and every one of your sons, and me because I know I have a life that was changed because of it. I thank you for that. I know you love us unconditionally. This is the kind of love Jesus loves us with and it is the kind of love we strive for here on this earth. I would like to say I have loved and turned into a man who constantly strives to be right and holy in God's eyes. Not only in His eyes, but in the eyes of those who love me and care for me like you do. I want you to know wherever I go or whatever I do, my love for you is as close to unconditional as Jesus' love for us, and I will always love you. I will never lose sight of my goals in life and also I will never lose sight of the most wonderful and long awaited goal, which is to get to Heaven. I would like to thank you for everything. You and Dad are the best parents.

Lovingly yours,

Your son,

Tim

Chapter Thirty-One

Tennessee

I will instruct you and teach you in the way you should go; I will guide you with My eye. **Psalm 32:8**

Toward the end of Andrew's twelfth grade year, he and Sandy got ready to go on a mission trip. They were all excited about it, and they were going to make this the best one ever! After they came home they graduated and began thinking about college. They both applied to Southern Adventist University in Tennessee, where Tim was for his last year. It seemed to us God was leading them there. They were both accepted.

Now Mark and I had a decision to make! He had been laid off from his job around the same time. Again, we found ourselves on our knees, asking for guidance. After much prayer, it seemed right to live near the college, and be there for Andrew's first year and Tim's graduation. I loved that idea, and Mark also loved the idea of leaving Maine and going south where it was much warmer! He always hated the cold weather, and now here was his opportunity. We had nothing to hold us, and we felt God's leading in a big way.

We packed our stuff and closed up the house and left for Tennessee! Some friends there invited us to come and stay with them. Then Tim found us a house to rent close to the college. It was a nice little house, and suited all our needs perfectly. Tim, Andrew, Mark, and I moved in, and the kids started their school year. Aaron and Sara came to stay for a brief visit. What a blessing to be all together again.

We also added a new member to the family. Tim brought home a puppy! She was adorable and he called her Zoë. She was into everything! Tim still has her, and his family just loves her.

The year was going great for the boys. Sandy lived in the girl's dorm, but she would come over and stay with us quite often. We were happy to have her. Mark found work at the elementary school close by, and I took care of an elderly lady. At times it was difficult since we still had to pay the mortgage on the mobile home, and we needed to save for a different car.

By December Mark received a letter from Maine telling him to come back to work. He loved Tennessee and his job at the school. Again, we found ourselves asking the Lord to show us His will. The old job paid well, and it would be financially wiser for him to return to Maine. Now I was alone with the kids and that was hard. I missed Mark and I knew he was missing me. The winter was cold. Tennessee was much warmer and I felt badly for him. I was counting the days until we would see each other again! Mark came back in May and we headed north, thanking God for His leading and for such a precious time with our family.

Now I was alone with the kids and that was hard. I missed Mark and I knew he was missing me

Chapter Thirty-Two
Opening Door of Providence

For whoever exalts himself will be abased, and he who humbles himself will be exalted. **Luke 14:11**

Andrew moved into the boy's dorm near the college. He was still working at the Food Corporation, sorting recycled boxes to help pay his tuition. Sandy worked there, too, for their first year of college, but when the school year ended, she went back to Maine. Problems had developed in their relationship, and they would no longer be seeing each other. Instead she went to KVTEC, which was a college in Maine near her home. From there she went to Atlantic Union College in Massachusetts, and eventually became a nurse. While at AUC, she met the young man who is now her husband.

Andrew continued to work at the box factory for two years. Then for his last year, the factory closed, and he found a job remodeling houses for the college. He thought he might make it his career, but I was glad when he chose not to. It would have meant hard, back-breaking work.

Toward the end of Andrew's last year, he was in one of his classes, when his professor asked him, "Do you have a job lined up after college?" He said, "Not really." He then asked him if he wanted a job and Andrew said, "Yes!" They went down to his office, and called the director of information technology at the conference. The director had been looking for an assistant for six months, and the professor told him he had the guy for the position! Andrew talked with the director on the phone, and went down that morning for an interview. They talked, they liked him, and they hired him!

Mark and I went to Andrew's graduation. Then we proceeded to pray about finding him a place to live, and soon God provided the perfect house for him. It was a townhouse, in a nice neighborhood, close to the Conference office where he was going to work. After he was all settled, we headed back home to Maine. Andrew worked at the Conference office for two and a half years, at which time the director moved away, and they began interviewing people to replace him. There were several people being interviewed and they encouraged Andrew to apply. Out of all the resumes they received, they liked Andrew's the best and said to him, "We want you to interview." He found himself before an imposing group of people. With shaking knees, he answered all their questions. He called us later, telling us we were talking with the new director!

At the conference office he met his future bride. Her name was Sheyla. At first they did not take any interest in each other, but over time a friendship began. They would go out together a lot, just enjoying each other's company. Andrew could see Jesus in Sheyla. She was bright, intelligent, and musical, had a strong caring for animals, and shared many of his interests. Love began to blossom between them. Andrew made a special dinner for her and asked her to marry him. She said, "Yes!" and he was very, very happy!! My life is now complete with the addition of my three daughters and all my grandchildren. "Thank you, Lord, for leading Andrew in the right direction, keeping him on the straight path, and blessing him with Sheyla."

(Andrew's Emails)

Mom,

I hope you have a wonderful 'Mother's Day. I want to thank you for always calling me and being the greatest mom in the world.

Love you forever,

Andrew

Mom,

I'm sure you miss being able to hold us boys like when we were babies. I still remember when I was too big to be carried. I always wanted you to pick me up. Thanks for trying anyway :). Don't worry. I won't ask you to pick me up anymore. Thanks for always loving us and praying for us. You have made us who we are today. I love you.

Happy Mother's Day!

Andrew

Mom,

I was just lying here on the floor listening to Christmas music and got to thinking about when I was little. I miss those times. I remember dancing around the living room with you, to that fast, crazy Jingle Bells song. Those were good times. I miss the family being together for Christmas, all of us being around our beautiful, big tree. It brings a tear to my eye to think about it.

Love and miss you,

Andrew

Chapter Thirty-Three

Life Changes

The Lord will give strength to His people; The Lord will bless His people with peace. **Psalm 29:11**

After coming back from Andrew's graduation, Mark and I had a fine summer. However, we were missing the kids terribly. I was feeling the grief of the empty nest, and Mark was getting more and more tired of Maine. His job was unstable, and we never knew when he would be laid off again. He kept an eye out for some work in the south, searching the web constantly, looking at temporary positions in different states. These jobs paid well, but it was just short term. We were not sure what we wanted to do, and kept praying. Fall came and went, then winter. We found ourselves still in Maine, cold and freezing.

Then, at Christmastime, Andrew came home for the holidays, and we went to visit my mom in Rhode Island. We had such fun visiting everyone. The morning we were going to leave, I was helping Mom with the morning chores. In the middle of making her bed, she suddenly fell over and screamed my name! I quickly cried for Mark. We helped her to a chair in the living room. She was having a hard time walking. Her speech was slurred, and we knew something bad had happened to her. She did not want us to call 911. Her mind was still sharp as a tack.

I contacted my sister, who is a registered nurse, and told her how Mom was, and could she please come over right away? She and her husband came over immediately, and when they assessed the situation, she told me Mom was suffering from a stroke, and we needed to get her to the hospital. We called an ambulance, and they came and took her. God's mercy manifested itself again. I can't imagine how it would have turned out if we had not stayed to help. That was just the beginning of my mom's illness. Life for her was going to be different. We would all need much strength for whatever lay ahead.

Chapter Thirty-Four

Caring for Mom

I lie awake and watch, I am like a sparrow alone on the housetop.
Psalm 102:7

After my mom's stroke, she had to stay in the hospital for about five weeks. Andrew, Mark, and I returned to Maine. When they released her, she still was unable to walk, but her speech had been restored. The doctor told her she would never walk again. I thought it would be best to go back to Rhode Island, stay with Mom at the apartment, and help her to recover. I would have to leave Mark in Maine.

It was hard going for her. We had to do physical therapy five times a day. She had a nice, long hallway outside her apartment with a hand bar across the wall. Every day, we went out there and practiced walking, first with the gait belt, and then she would do it by herself. I also did a series of exercises with her. That was such a challenge. Then, ever so slowly, she began to get her strength back. Her walking was improving, despite what the doctors had said! The Lord often has different plans for us than what the world expects.

It seemed I was watching and waiting for something to happen, but I didn't know what it was. I knew God was in charge

I stayed with Mom for three months. It seemed to me they were the longest three months without Mark. In addition to everything, 'Mom's cataracts were growing. Her walking would have been much better if she could only see. I was having such a tough time with her! The possibility of falling and getting hurt was constant. She hated using the walker and was not careful with it. She was improving, but not enough to ever leave her alone. I prayed and read to her from the Bible each morning.

Not a moment went by that I did not feel lonely and lost without my husband. It seemed I was watching and waiting for something to happen, but I didn't know what it was. I knew God was in charge. He wanted me to help my mom, but it was unbelievably hard for me. I prayed constantly for the strength and the patience I needed, to do my part, no matter how long it took.

Chapter Thirty-Five

The New Job

It shall come to pass that before they call, I will answer; and while they are still speaking, I will hear. **Isaiah 65:24**

By the middle of March things were still not changing. I was doing the same routine with Mom, praying every day God would show me what to do next. Then Mark called me and said there was a job opening in Virginia! Northrop Grumman was looking for a ship designer. He was very interested, and after we prayed about it, he applied on-line. The shipyard called him and said they would fly him out for an interview. When he arrived it was seventy-seven degrees! That was enough for Mark! He called me and said he was hired, and we would be moving by the end of the month! I talked with Mom, and told her she'd have to live with us until she was able to be on her own again. She understood, but oh my, now I had to figure out what to do with her because I needed to go back home to get ready to move. It seemed like just one big challenge after another. Everything was overwhelming, but I knew God would take care of it all. Mark got that job for a reason, and I just had to trust in Him to take care of the rest.

I made phone calls to my brother in North Carolina, and asked him if he could take Mom while I went home to pack. It would involve traveling sixteen hours for him to come and get her. He said he'd have to talk with his wife because they had a little one to take care of at home, and it might end up being too much to deal with Mom as well. After discussing it together, they said they could have her for a month. This would give us time to go and get settled in Virginia before we brought her to live with us.

I was getting excited now, knowing I'd finally be going home to my husband! Thank you, God, for such a big answer to my prayers! I was counting the days until my brother and his family would be arriving. Mom was walking with just a cane now, but she hated that cane. She'd put it over her head and go too fast. Her mind couldn't tell her feet to slow down, and she'd almost walk into the walls! We would both find ourselves laughing at how funny she looked! In a little while she was able to go slower.

Then came the day my brother was to arrive. We packed 'Mom's things. It was hard for her to let go of her independence because she knew in her heart there might not be a coming back, but for now, we were taking one step at a time. First, we had to get her somewhere safe, which would enable me to go home to Mark and face what was happening there. Thank God for family.

Everyone arrived around the same time. It was terrific to see them all, especially my Mark! We had a joyful visit, then said our "goodbyes," assuring Mom we would come and get her as soon as we got settled in Virginia. The Lord had met the needs of each one of us.

Chapter Thirty-Six

Leaving Maine

But you, be strong and do not let your hands be weak, for your work shall be rewarded! 2 Chronicles 15:7

It was fantastic to be alone with Mark again, even if it was to be a short time. We found out the shipyard would be sending a moving company to pack all of our belongings. Wow! However, it was very hard to let someone come into my home and pack my stuff. Instead, I started to do my own sorting to get it ready which was just as tiring as doing all the packing!

When the packers arrived they went through everything, with me supervising, of course. There was much to do! They took a whole day to pack and then left, saying they would be back again the next day to load it all in the truck. I could not believe that even my old upright piano was coming with us!

Company frequently came over to say farewell to us. Many friends had been made during our sixteen years in Maine. The hardest part of moving was leaving everyone. On the last day before the move, the house was just about empty. I was home alone, doing the final cleaning, when Michael and Maria, close friends of ours, came around dinner time; almost time for Mark to come home from work. We decided when Mark came, we'd spend our last night together eating out at our favorite place. They made such delicious sandwiches there! It was a terrific visit, reminiscing, going over all the years we had with each other, all the ups and downs with our kids, who had gone to the same Christian school together. What fun we had talking and laughing! Those times will always be treasured.

The next morning we headed out to Virginia!! The company had provided us with an apartment to stay in, giving us three months to find a place of our own. All expenses were going to be paid, including our food and storing our things. It almost felt like the honeymoon we had never been able to afford!

The temporary apartments were spacious, clean, and furnished with quality items, everything we needed. It was located on the second floor, which would make it difficult for Mom. We needed to pick her up by the end of April. This was the end of March, leaving us only a little time to find another place. Meanwhile we cherished our time together, alone at last in Virginia, the warm state we have come to love.

Chapter Thirty-Seven

Waiting on the Lord

The light shines through the darkness, and the darkness can never extinguish it. **John 1:5**

We were looking constantly for a place of our own, praying hard to the Lord for His guidance. The month was going rapidly, and we were not finding anything suitable. God was constantly answering, "No" or "Wait." Stress was building because we had to go and get Mom soon! We called the company and explained to them how my mom had experienced a stroke and was going to live with us. As a result, she would not be able to climb any stairs. Thankfully, they understood and gave us another apartment on the first floor. It was just as beautiful as the first one.

Then came the day we went to get Mom. North Carolina, where my brother lived, was only a five-hour drive. When we arrived at my brother's home, we found Mom excited and ready to leave! We spent the night there, and the next morning we were on our way, realizing life as we once knew it would no longer be the same.

It was not easy caring for Mom. She had a strong will, especially where food was concerned. She loved to do her own cooking. The company was paying for our food, and we enjoyed going out to eat, but she hated all the food the restaurants served and would not eat with us. There were many arguments until I could not deal with it anymore.

Handling every situation demanded much prayer. Arguing all the time was not being a good witness to her. I wanted Mom to see the love of God through me and that wasn't happening. I thought, "What would Jesus do?" He would respect her choices and let her learn from them. Peace came to me. She would eat when she got hungry. Then life became much more pleasant with her. "Thank you, Lord, for giving me my mom." Continuing to learn these hard lessons will mold and shape me into the loving and patient person You intend for me to be."

We were still searching for a place to live. The company kept moving us from one first floor apartment to another and it was becoming very apparent Mom needed her own space. One day we all went for a drive, just looking at all the lovely neighborhoods in Yorktown. We came across this home for rent, parked in front of it, and said how much we would love to live in something like that! On the "For Rent" sign in the yard was a number to call. I quickly got on my cell phone. A kind woman answered and said she would send me pictures of the inside over the computer, and if we liked what we saw, to give her husband a call.

When we checked our computer, we were very interested! Her husband showed us the house and we signed the contract. Mom would have her own living room, bedroom, and bath and we would have some much-needed privacy as well. We had moved five times, but God had provided this house just for us. What a blessing!

Chapter Thirty-Eight

A Home at Last

Wait on the Lord; be of good courage, and He shall strengthen your heart; wait, I say, on the Lord! **Psalm 27:14**

The three months the company had given us to find a place had come and gone. We found ourselves in the month of June paying extra for our storage. Mom's apartment was still full of all her things. She hired Tim to go and clean it out, and bring everything down to Virginia. This caused us to have to pay for another storage unit. We were definitely ready for a bigger place!

When moving day arrived, we called the storage companies and told them to bring everything to our new address. Now Mom did not feel quite so lost. She had familiar things around her, making it look more like home. Praise God!

Mom was not the only one who enjoyed seeing her things again. Mark and I felt the same way! It had been almost four months since everything was packed and hauled away by the moving trucks in Maine. Now we had to face the task of unpacking and decorating. Not easy to do with two women in the house having entirely different views on things! Mom was the decorator, I was not, but I knew what I didn't want. We finally found agreement and the house looked sweet. Mom appreciated her space and we appreciated ours. We were thanking God every day for such a lovely home. We even put a hot tub in the back yard. We had everything to make us happy.

During this time, we took a trip in March to see our Aaron, Sara, and grandson in Germany, whom we had only seen on the computer with the web cam. My brother said he would take care of Mom again while we were away. We met all of Sara's family for the first time and saw many interesting sites. Then we came home, got Mom, and settled into the task of keeping house and enjoying each other.

We thought we would be there forever. Sorry to say, it was not to be. One day the landlord called us and said the owner of the house was thinking about selling his home. When we heard that news we were devastated. The "For Sale" sign went up, exactly one year from when we had arrived. There were many people coming to look at the house and it sold quickly. The landlord had given us the option to buy it, but we did not have enough money at the time. Now we had the horrible task of looking for another place to live. Again, we prayed for God's help to guide us as to what we should do next. Thank you, Lord, for teaching us a long time ago to trust, and we knew You would not fail us.

Chapter Thirty-Nine

On the Move Again

A man's heart plans his way, but the Lord directs his steps.
Proverbs 16:9

With heavy hearts we prayed to our mighty God in heaven to show us the way. We just could not imagine finding another place like the one we were in.

We contacted a real estate agent. Jennifer came to the house right away, and Mom and I loved her from the start. She was determined to help us. We checked out different places, but nothing seemed right. Then the suggestion was made to buy a modular home. We could be in a nice place again and this time it would be ours. Her brother-in-law sold them, and he told us we'd have to start by buying some land. We knew that was not going to be easy because land was expensive, but we started looking, leaving the outcome in God's hands.

We began searching on the computer and found a nice piece in the town of Surry. We called Jennifer and she made all the arrangements for us to go and see it. This included a ferry ride which was fun for all of us, and would make living in Surry a unique experience! After looking at the land, we put down a deposit. There would also be the added expense of putting in a well and septic system, and lots of trees would have to be cut down. The appropriate people came and began measuring and testing.

Meanwhile, we started picking out our modular home with Jennifer's brother-in-law. What fun! We chose the colors and flooring, customizing it all and dreaming of having this home someday. This was a long process, especially the deal with the land. Then we were informed we would have to move before our new place would be ready, causing us to need a temporary apartment to stay in.

On one of our "driving around days," the thought came to us to try and find an apartment like the ones the company had put us up in the year before. There were many to choose from. We asked how much the rent was and found out they were too expensive for us to even think about. We never realized how much the company paid to provide one of those! There were some suitable ones way across town which were not as nice as the expensive ones, but we rented one anyway. There were also some apartments near our neighborhood we had overlooked. Out of curiosity we stopped in to inquire about them and found they had a first-floor apartment available! It would not be as much effort and stress to make the move.

We called the manager of the apartments across town, knowing our deposit would probably not be returned, but praying for God to intervene on our behalf. He did! There was a company with a "pod" to store things in and they'd leave it in our driveway while we proceeded to move things into it, even our big, heavy piano!

Mark also built this long trailer on wheels which we used to move our remaining things. Pretty cool! We could even walk with it down the street to the apartment. I have to tell you we looked pretty funny with our belongings on the trailer, but we didn't care. At least we had a place to live. We met some nice neighbors while pulling it. They were walking their dogs and we were walking our furniture! The apartment proved to be too small for all of our things, forcing us to rent a nearby storage place, but it was okay since we knew this situation was only going to be temporary.

Chapter Forty

The Home God Chose

Come and see the works of God; He is awesome in His doing toward the sons of men. **Psalm 66:5**

The small apartment was quite a change from our large, roomy home. We even lost our hot tub as a result of having nowhere to put it. I was discouraged. Mom still had her own bedroom and bath, for which we were very thankful. It was the middle of June when we settled in. All Mom and I could chat about every day was the modular home and how exciting it would be to have it. The months kept going by, and we were constantly talking to Jennifer's brother-in-law about it, but our piece of land was not panning out. When we had drawn up the papers, it was with the stipulation we would be able to drill a well. It turned out it was not possible which ended our contract. Another disappointment!

> *It seemed I was watching and waiting for something to happen, but I didn't know what it was. I knew God was in charge*

The fall season was coming on quickly and we felt trapped in this little apartment. We called Jennifer again to help us find a home to buy this time, instead of renting. She took Mom and I out every day looking, but nothing was within our price range. Sometimes Mark would be with us when he was not at work. It was all getting very disheartening. We were on our knees praying for God to lead us to the right home. I repeatedly said that when we saw the right place, I would know it. God would tell me. We saw house after house, and I was not impressed with any of them. Even the suitable ones didn't have the sense of "right" for us.

Then one day Jennifer called and said she had found a home in Newport News. It had a converted garage which could be turned into a living room for Mom. The house was not for sale yet, but was going up shortly. The owners were moving because the military had stationed them somewhere else. She gave us the address and told us to go and check it out without going inside. When I heard it was in Newport News, my heart sank! All of our apartments and the nice house we lived in were in Yorktown. We just loved this little town. The crime rate was low, not like what I had heard concerning Newport News, but we thought we should go and check out the house anyway, despite my apprehensions.

As we drew closer to the area where the house was, my heart was getting excited. The neighborhood was attractive and I knew this was it. I could hardly contain myself! When I actually saw the place, I was impressed again, this was the one! We stopped in front and called Jennifer, telling her to draw up the contract. We had found the house God wanted us to live in! We didn't even know what the inside looked like, but knowing God wanted us to buy this one was all that mattered. She said she would try to make it possible for us to see the inside soon and talk to the owners. We went back to our little apartment full of hope.

Chapter Forty-One

Transformation Needed

And all these blessings shall come upon you, and overtake you, because you obey the voice of the Lord your God. **Deuteronomy 28:2**

With rising anticipation Mark, my mom, and I drove over to Newport News again. We discovered the house was only ten minutes away from Colonial Williamsburg; a fascinating place to visit with much to see. I got on the Internet later in the evening and found that the area of Newport News where we would be moving was a safe neighborhood, confirming my conviction that God had chosen this house for us.

When we went to have a closer look at the place, the wife was home with her three little ones. Seeing the inside was a letdown. It was in need of serious cosmetic repair. Trying to count our blessings, we were thankful it was just puttying holes, painting walls, and cleaning up. The converted garage wasn't going to work as a living room and Mark preferred we make it into a garage again. We went out to the large backyard and found a deck which was a big surprise! The outside was also neglected, but nothing we couldn't handle. Despite all the work, I still felt God was leading us to buy this place, and I told the wife we really wanted it.

We heard from Jennifer a few days later, and she said we could have the house as is! We said, "No problem," and we signed the papers. Our closing was October 5th, but even after the closing we wouldn't be able to move in. The owners had to wait until the military let them go which would be December 5th, meaning we'd be spending our first Christmas there. We began counting the days until the move!

When December arrived we were ready! Our Mustang became a moving van and we made several trips to the house from Yorktown. On one of those trips, we met our new neighbor, Gary. He was very generous and offered his big trailer to move all of our stuff! God provided helpful neighbors on every side. The company was notified to bring the pod. We emptied it, carrying everything into the house, but not unpacking anything as we needed to knock down walls and finish the other repairs first. My mom looked lost in this big mess.

We had to change all the doors and fix some electrical work. After exhausting effort, it was done. When we first saw the inside, I didn't understand why God wanted us to have this house. Now, I couldn't imagine being anywhere else. The transformation was remarkable.

It reminds me of what our loving God does for us. When He first sees us, we are nothing to look at. We are full of disgusting holes and in need of cosmetic repairs. We too are a big mess, but God looks beyond all of it and notices the wonderful possibilities in us. He gets excited and thinks, here is someone with potential!

He sees past our brokenness and starts to go to work, never getting discouraged, but ever so lovingly begins the task of filling in the holes, the wounds sin has made, and covering us with His righteousness, cleaning us from the inside out. He knocks down the structures we have built in our lives to protect ourselves and gratify our needs. They are no longer necessary and He builds new structures to protect us and grant our heart's desires, restoring us to His original design.

We come to Him just as we are. He receives us and the process begins. It is a process involving time, effort and patience on His part and ours. He gives us friends and helpers as we journey along, making our progress easier. New doors begin to open and He transforms our thoughts, emotions, and goals. His will for us is that we become someone beautiful to behold. When He gets through, He stands back to admire His handiwork and thinks, "Wow! This is good, very good."Romans 12:2 says, "And do not be conformed to this world, but be transformed by the renewing of your mind, that you may prove what is that good and acceptable and perfect will of God."

Chapter Forty-Two

Mom

For this is God, our God forever and ever, He will be our guide, even to death. **Psalm 48:14**

As I look around me, I am amazed how far the Lord has taken me in my long journey. It has not been an easy road, but a rather bumpy one, with many challenges along the way. We still have Mom, after six and a half years. She has had a bumpy road along with us. Her health has grown worse as she has grown older. One day she told me she did not feel well. When the doctor checked her, he found she was a diabetic. What a change for both of us. Mom would have to learn a whole new way of eating and I would have to learn to test blood sugar and give insulin shots, increasing her dependence on me, which was discouraging to her.

She still could not see with the cataracts in her eyes which was making us both miserable. I was happy when she announced she wanted those out. I proceeded to call the appropriate doctor and make the appointments. The left eye was the one with the biggest problem. It had become very thick and was hard to remove. After the surgery, for the first time in many years, she saw again. She was praising God for this big miracle! Unfortunately, that eye became infected and took her eyesight away. I prayed every day for her eye to get better and every day God said, "No." I didn't understand why God would allow this to happen. I am still learning that all things work together for the good. Afflictions teach us important lessons (Romans 8:28; Corinthians 12:8).[5, 6] Now Mom is doing a little better. She has adjusted to everything and seems to be much happier with us.

(Mom's Letters)

Dear Nancy,

I want to thank you for being there for me when I had my stroke. I was so grateful for you when I came back to my apartment because I still could not walk or do things by myself, and I know I would have had to go to a nursing home without your care. You were the one who taught me how to function normally again, spending countless hours working with me to gain my strength. I couldn't have done it without you. You even left Mark for three months to help me!

Love you always,

Mom

Dear Mark,

I want you to know I loved you from the beginning and value all you have done for me, always bringing Nancy and the kids to visit, no matter how far it was to travel. Whenever I asked you to do anything, there was never any hesitation on your part. I also want to say thank you for sharing your home with me all these years. You never once have complained about me and you treat me like I was your mother. You will always be like a son.

Love you,

Mom

Chapter Forty-Three

Forgiveness

Who is a God like you, pardoning iniquity and passing over the transgression of the remnant of His heritage? He does not retain His anger forever, because He delights in mercy. He will again have compassion on us, and will subdue our iniquities. You will cast all our sins into the depths of the sea. **Micah 7:18, 19**

In the first twenty years of my life I experienced much hurt, then anger, and finally forgiveness toward many people. Uncle Sandy was constantly at our home, making life more difficult for all of us. Mom seemed happy enough with him being there because she had someone to talk to. However, there were times she was upset with him too, as he would occasionally encourage my dad to go to the bars. He was also contributing to my father's anger. Dad would come home from work and find them laughing, knowing this had been going on all day. Jealousy was in his heart, but he never said anything for he loved his brother. My sister Millie and I were not pleased about it at all. We felt if Uncle Sandy would just leave us alone we would be a happier family. Often I retreated to my bedroom feeling a hate for him.

One time my mom was desperate and decided she would be better off dead. I was upset, hurt, and angry with her. How could she want to die and leave us five children with my drunken dad?! I surely did not understand her viewpoint of what was happening. The hurt was seeded deep within her, and she was blinded by it. She did try to end her life, but I thank God He was there to intervene.

I think back during those years of my childhood and remember when my dad would be drinking in the bars and not come home. Like my sister, I had many nights when tension and anxiety drove me to live on aspirin to calm me down. I thought if dad would only not come home, things would be better or if he would even die, our world would be a nicer, more peaceful place to live.

As my parents grew older they changed. They were treating each other better and the accusations were decreasing, but the drinking and smoking on my dad's part hadn't changed. My mom still could not get a restful sleep, always wondering if he would burn the house down in the middle of the night. As I grew older, Jesus was showing me how to understand and forgive them. I was praying to become more like Him and He was changing me. After all, doesn't He forgive us when we sincerely ask Him? I knew in my heart, if I was to be like Him, I would have to forgive and bury all the deepest hurts and anger toward them in the sea, forever. I prayed every day, and little by little my love was starting to outweigh the hate. I began to feel sorry for them and longed for their salvation.

When I had my children I felt it was important for them to know their grandparents. I made an effort to bring them there no matter how far away we lived. There were challenges while we were visiting, like their choice of movies and the smoking and drinking. My dad tried to listen to what I wanted, but it was hard for him sometimes. My mom didn't smoke, and I found she was much easier to talk to about all of this. She understood my requests. As my children grew older they accepted their grandparents for who they were. Having their grandchildren visit was a real blessing and I believe it helped them in many ways.

When my dad got sick and was dying, I prayed God would heal him and I thought how ironic this was. Years ago I had prayed for his death and now I was praying God would let him live! What a difference when we have Jesus in our hearts. Then I got afraid because maybe Dad would go back to being the same old person he used to be if God healed him. Instead, I began to pray for God's will to be done, not mine. I truly believe when my dad died he gave his heart to the Lord and I will see him again when Jesus comes.

I am thankful God showed me how to forgive. When we harbor hate toward those who do us wrong, and we don't want to forgive, something

> *I knew in my heart, if I was to be like Him, I would have to forgive and bury all the deepest hurts and anger toward them in the sea, forever. I prayed every day, and little by little my love was starting to outweigh the hate*

happens inside of us. It is like a cancer that grows and grows until the love we could have toward one another dies. Only through persevering prayer can we let go of the anger, fear, and hurt. God comes in and heals and removes all of it, and replaces it with peace and love. Philippians 4:7 says, "And the peace of God, which surpasses all understanding, will guard your hearts and minds through Christ Jesus."

Epilogue

Then the King shall say to those on His right hand, Come, you blessed of My Father, inherit the kingdom prepared for you from the foundation of the world. **Matthew 25:34**

The question I asked in my childhood, "Why do we have to face heartaches, challenges, and sufferings?" has been answered as I learned that there is a great struggle going on in this world between good and evil for the hearts and minds of men. The angel closest to God in heaven allowed jealousy and pride to take root in his heart. He chose to deny God's love and began to misrepresent who God was, with profound subtlety. Tragically and for no valid reason at all, one third of the angels believed him (Revelation 12:4).[7] A crises developed in Heaven, and despite all the reasoning, evidence, and love shown to him by God, he chose to believe his own lies. War broke out and Satan found himself wanting to get revenge on God by causing His children on the earth to sin and be separated from God like he was (Revelation 12:7–9).[8] He is the originator of all the troubles in this world. He is here, lurking around every corner, causing disruption all around us. Every time we have a choice to make, we can be sure Satan is trying to influence us in the wrong direction (1 Peter 5:7–9).[9]

God will not force us to love Him. He has created us with a free will and respects our choices. Satan's lies and misrepresentations about Him need time to be revealed for what they are. If God had destroyed him when he first began to deceive, we would all serve Him out of fear rather than love.

This is why evil has been allowed to remain for a season. We have to watch and pray faithfully for ourselves or we will fall into Satan's evil trap. When Jesus returns there will be a day of judgment (2 Peter 3:7–14).[10] Satan wants us to lose our lives as he will on that day. God wants us to live for eternity with Him (Ezekiel 28: 13–19).[11] He loves us so much.

I found every time I prayed and asked for God's guidance and protection, He was there. The biggest lesson God had to teach me was how to be kind and unselfish to those around me. I was self-centered and wanted my own way. Relationships were hard as I was very difficult to get along with. During the first year of our marriage I said many cruel things to Mark, wanting his undivided attention; hollering, screaming, and throwing things at him. I loved my Lord and had chosen to follow Him at a young age, but there was still a dark side of me that wouldn't leave easily, without help. Through all of this I saw the love of God in my sweet husband. He was patient and never spoke an unkind word to me.

Sometimes during my afflictions, Satan would tempt me to blame God for what I was going through. No matter how many horrible things I experienced, I could not curse God because I knew it was Satan who was really to blame. In addition, I felt at times I was bad and did not deserve anything but death, which is the truth, but God so loved you and me that He gave His only begotten Son, that as we believe in Him, we will not perish but have everlasting life (John 3:16).

I loved my Lord for paying the wages of my sinfulness and I wanted to be faithful to Him. Studying God's Word is crucial to overcoming. His words must be stored in our minds for Him to bring them back to us when we need help. My strength increased as I read His Word, prayed constantly, and claimed the promises of His acceptance and power to keep me from sinning. God was also showing me through my husband and children how to love and live a righteous life. Little by little my character was being transformed. I was learning to be more like Jesus.

Today, I am not perfect by any means, but I know when Jesus looks at me, He is not seeing a terrible person. He is seeing His child. I know He is always standing right beside me, longing to take me in His loving arms, guiding me until He comes in the clouds of glory to take me home to a better land. That is the day I am waiting for. Praise God! I am a child of the King!

After

Light after darkness,
Gain after loss,
Strength after weakness,
Crown after cross,
Sweet after bitter,
Hope after fears,
Home after wandering,
Praise after tears,
Sheaves after sowing,
Sun after rain,
Sight after mystery,
Peace after pain,
Joy after sorrow,
Calm after blast,
Rest after weariness,
Sweet rest at last,
Near after distance,
Gleam after gloom,
Love after loneliness,
Life after tomb,
After deep sorrow,
Rapture of bliss,
Right was the pathway,
Leading to this!
Author Unknown

The Better Land

And I saw a new heaven and a new earth: for the first heaven and the first earth were passed away; and there was no more sea.

And I John saw the holy city, New Jerusalem, coming down from God out of heaven, prepared as a bride adorned for her husband.

And I heard a great voice out of heaven saying, Behold, the tabernacle of God is with men, and he will dwell with them, and they shall be his people, and God Himself shall be with them, and be their God.

And God shall wipe away all tears from their eyes; and there shall be no more death, neither sorrow, nor crying, neither shall there be any more pain: for the former things are passed away.

And He that sat upon the throne said, Behold, I make all things new. And he said unto me, Write: for these words are true and faithful. (Revelation 21:1–5, KJV)

And he shewed me a pure river of water of life, clear as crystal, proceeding out of the throne of God and of the Lamb.

In the midst of the street of it, and on either side of the river, was there the tree of life, which bare twelve manner of fruits, and yielded her fruit every month: and the leaves of the tree were for the healing of the nations.

And there shall be no more curse: but the throne of God and of the Lamb shall be in it; and his servants shall serve him.

And they shall see His face; and his name shall be in their foreheads.

And there shall be no night there; and they need no candle, neither light of the sun; for the Lord God giveth them light: and they shall reign forever and ever.

And, behold, I am coming quickly; and my reward is with me, to give every man according as his work shall be.

Blessed are those who do his commandments that they may have right to the tree of life, and may enter in through the gates into the city.

And the Spirit and the bride say, Come. And let him that heareth say, Come. And let him that is athirst come. And whosoever will, let him take the water of life freely. (Revelation 22:1–5, 12, 14, 17, KJV)

Scriptural Index

NKJV and KJV

1. Exodus 20:8–11 (NKJV)

Remember the Sabbath day, to keep it holy. Six days you shall labor, and do all your work. But the seventh day is the Sabbath of the Lord your God. In it you shall do no work: you, nor your son, nor your daughter, nor your manservant, nor your maidservant, nor your cattle, nor your stranger that is within your gates. For in six days the Lord made the heavens and the earth, the sea, and all that in them is, and rested the seventh day. Therefore the Lord blessed the Sabbath day and hallowed it.

2. John 14:15, 21 (NKJV)

If you love Me, keep My commandments. He who has My commandments and keeps them, it is he who loves Me. And he who loves Me will be loved by My Father, and I will love him, and will manifest Myself to him.

3. Daniel 12:1 (NKJV)

And at that time Michael shall stand up, the great prince who stands watch over the sons of your people; and there shall be a time of trouble, such as never was since there was a nation even to that time. And at that time your people shall be delivered. Everyone who is found written in the book.

4. Psalms 36:5, 6 (NKJV)

Your mercy, O Lord, is in the heavens, and Your faithfulness reaches to the clouds. Your righteousness is like the great mountains; Your judgments are a great deep; O Lord, You preserve man and beast.

5. Romans 8:28 (NKJV)

And we know that all things work together for good to those who love God, to those who are the called according to His purpose.

6. 2 Corinthians 12:8, 9 (NKJV)

Concerning this thing I pleaded with the Lord three times that it might depart from me. And He said to me, "My grace is sufficient for you, for My strength is made perfect in weakness." Therefore most gladly I would rather boast in my infirmities, that the power of Christ may rest upon me.

7. Revelation 12:4 (NKJV)

His tail drew a third of the stars of heaven and threw them to the earth. And the dragon stood before the woman who was ready to give birth, to devour her Child as soon as it was born.

8. Revelation 12:7–9 (NKJV)

And war broke out in heaven: Michael and his angels fought against the dragon; and the dragon and his angels fought, but they did not prevail, nor was a place found for them in heaven any longer. So the great dragon was cast out, that serpent of old, called the Devil and Satan, who deceives the whole world; he was cast to the earth, and his angels were cast out with him.

9. 1 Peter 5: 7–9 (NKJV)

Casting all your care upon Him; for He cares for you. Be sober, be vigilant; because your adversary the devil walks about like a roaring lion, seeking whom he may devour. Resist him, steadfast in the faith, knowing that the same sufferings are experienced by your brotherhood in the world.

10. 2 Peter 3:7–13 (NKJV)

But the heavens and the earth which now exist are kept in store by the same word, reserved for fire until the day of judgment and perdition of ungodly men. But, beloved, do not forget this one thing, that with the Lord one day is as a thousand years, and a thousand years as one day. The Lord is not slack concerning His promise, as some count slackness, but is long suffering toward us, not willing that any should perish but that all should come to repentance. But the day of the Lord will come as a thief in the night, in which the heavens shall pass away with a great noise, and the elements will melt with fervent heat; both the earth and the works that are in it will be burned up. Therefore, since all these things will be dissolved, what manner of persons ought you to be in all holy conduct and godliness, looking for and hastening the coming of the day of God, because of which the heavens will be dissolved being on fire, and the elements will melt with fervent heat? Nevertheless we, according to His promise, look for new heavens and a new earth in which righteousness dwells.

11. Ezekiel 28:13–19 (KJV)

Thou hast been in Eden, the garden of God; every precious stone was thy covering, the sardius, topaz, and the diamond, the beryl, the onyx, and the jasper, the sapphire, the emerald, and the carbuncle, and gold: the workmanship of thy tabrets and of thy pipes was prepared in thee in the day that thou wast created. Thou art the anointed cherub that covereth; and I have set thee so: thou wast upon the holy mountain of God; thou hast walked up and down in the midst of the stones of fire. Thou wast perfect in thy ways from the day that thou wast created, till iniquity was found in thee. By the multitude of thy merchandise they have filled the midst of thee with violence, and thou hast sinned: therefore I will cast thee as profane out of the mountain of God: and I will destroy thee, O covering cherub, from the midst of the stones of fire. Thine heart was lifted up because of thy beauty; thou hast corrupted thy wisdom by reason of thy brightness: I will cast thee to the ground; I will lay thee before kings, that they may behold thee. Thou hast defiled thy sanctuaries by the multitude of thine iniquities, by the iniquity of thy traffic; therefore will I bring forth a fire from the midst of thee, it shall devour thee, and I will bring thee to ashes upon the earth in the sight of all them that behold thee. All they that know thee among the people shall be astonished at thee: thou shalt be a terror, and never shalt thou be anymore.

Bible Study Guides

Voice of Prophecy

Bible School

PO Box 999
Loveland, CO 80539-0999

bibleschools.com
discoverschool@vop.com

Faith for Today

P.O. Box 1000
Thousand Oaks, CA 91359
[888]943-0062

www.faithfortoday.tv

Recommended Reading

Steps to Christ

By Ellen G. White
Review and Herald Publishing Association
Washington, DC 20039-0555
Hagerstown, MD 21740
Copyright1892

The Great Controversy

By Ellen G. White
Pacific Press Publishing Association
Copyright1950

Desire of Ages

By Ellen G. White
Pacific Press Publishing Association
Copyright1898

The Bible Story

By Arthur S. Maxwell
Review and Herald Publishing Association
Copyright1994

About the Author

Nancy Berthiaume LaPierre (1954 —) was born in Woonsocket, Rhode Island, to French Canadian parents. She grew up in R.I. in an unstable, alcoholic home. She married Mark LaPierre in 1974. Her first child was born three years later (1977). Mark and Nancy were blessed with two more beautiful baby boys. She was determined to raise them in a loving, stable, Christian home, something she never experienced herself.

She realized how God took care of her and her brothers and sisters while growing up, and how He is still watching over her. She survived the challenges of raising three children in a school bus for the sake of Christian education.

God has shown her how to forgive her parents and found herself taking care of her mom after she had suffered a stroke. She had the privilege of caring for her for seven years, up until her death in 2010.

She is now enjoying life with her children and grandchildren, every chance she can get. She shared her story in this book, in hopes to bless others that might be going through or have gone through similar trials.

Other Books by the Author

God's Power Revealed Through Prayer

Courage for the Soul of the Caregiver

Journey to a Better Land: Inspirational Gems (Three-Volume Audio Book)

To order these books and to find out more about the author, please go to www.nblbooks.com or https://1ref.us/zzzzzz. Also available at fine bookstores everywhere and at www.TEACHServices.com.

Reviews

"*Journey to a Better Land* was excellent. Once I started reading it, I couldn't put it down except to sleep at night. The author's husband, Mark, is my cousin and I now feel that I know him and his family better than I know a lot of people. I was impressed how Nancy and Mark and their three sons survived so many hardships and struggled through so much with the strength of God helping them through it all. It was very inspiring. I am anxiously awaiting Nancy's next book."

— *Linda Davidson*

"This is such an inspirational book. Nancy and her family were in such peril and with the love of God, found a way out. *Journey to a Better Land* is a book for everyone. If you are hurting, sad, depressed, or dealing with the unimaginable, this book will be a guide out of the darkness. I could not put this book down; it was a true page turner! It gave me hope and I felt truly immersed in the story. Thank you, Nancy, for writing this book of hope and love. There really is light at the end of even the darkest night— nothing is hopeless. God bless you."

— *Susan Dreesen, caregiver*

"This is an amazing, true story of one family's search for meaning and triumph even in adversity. This engrossing book invites us all to join Nancy's family and experience the same transformative journey."

— *Kristina Zanotti, Esq.*

Through the eyes of an 11-year-old...

"*Journey to a Better Land* is such an interesting book. The author of this book attends my church and she was surprised that I enjoyed the book. It was written to inspire adults. In this case it was different. Since I am a child, I took it into a perspective of an adventure. It's like in children's books there might be a prince who has to fight dragons and go through obstacles to get to the princess. This is how the book appeared to me. Mrs. Nancy had to work through the hard times. It seemed as if nothing would ever go right and there were many times of disappointment and times of despair. But anything and everything is possible through God, and Mrs. Nancy really did believe that was true. I really enjoyed the book and I hope others will too!!"

—*Kayla Toliver*

TEACH Services, Inc.
PUBLISHING

We invite you to view the complete
selection of titles we publish at:
www.TEACHServices.com

We encourage you to write us
with your thoughts about this,
or any other book we publish at:
info@TEACHServices.com

TEACH Services' titles may be purchased in
bulk quantities for educational, fund-raising,
business, or promotional use.
bulksales@TEACHServices.com

Finally, if you are interested in seeing
your own book in print, please contact us at:
publishing@TEACHServices.com
We are happy to review your manuscript at no charge.

www.ingramcontent.com/pod-product-compliance
Lightning Source LLC
Chambersburg PA
CBHW071625170426
43195CB00038B/2127